INTRODUCTION

People are funny. Their languages funny too. To those of us who have da[b]. a bit in linguistics, some of the most fascinating aspects of a language are its idioms, adages, sayings and phrases that cannot be literally translated nor can they be found in books that teach. Some of them are witty, some paradoxical, some are strange, some wise. Literal translations of some of those is virtually impossible, but it is a source of amusement because another language is created whose images are unique.

This little book then is just to share those fun and amusing moments and perhaps teach a bit. — V.V. Elliott.

* ALSO: FORWARD - PREFACE - PROLOGUE

A NOTE TO THOSE WHO ARE FLUENT IN - NOT TO
MENTION THEY KNOW WELL - BOTH LANGUAGES

HEREIN YOU WILL UNDOUBTEDLY FIND INTERPRETATIONS
WITH WHICH YOU WILL NOT AGREE, JUST AS I HAVE
FOUND FREQUENTLY IN OTHER WORKS.
WELL THAT'S THE WAY THE BALL BOUNCES.
IF YOU DISAGREE VIOLENTLY, THEN WRITE
YOUR OWN BOOK!

INSTRUCTIONS
WARNINGS AND DISCLAIMERS

This book is divided into many parts.
I tried to make some sense of it, but couldn't.
It does contain some things you may want to
tell your waiter in a taverna, your co-travelers
in a packed trolley-bus in Athens in the summer,
your friendly taxi driver, or a public servant,
should you have the misfortune to need him-her.

Throughout the book you will find notations
footnotes e.t.c. about the circumstances where
some of these sayings may be appropriate to
use - culturally that is. Care is taken that your
response will not create a riot, nor will it
endanger you physically. Be forewarned
however, that any such directive should
not be taken too seriously as there are
too many exceptions to the rule. After all
remember, you are in Greece.

11

A GUIDE TO PRONUNCIATION (GOOD LUCK)

There are 24 letters in the Greek Alphabet. Some of them are redundant for no apparent reason and are pronounced identically. (in other words they are homophones, for those of you who care to be technical.)

They are : eta H, η ⎫
      iota I, ι ⎬ pronounced EE
      eepsilon Y, υ ⎭ as in f<u>EE</u>

isn't that easy?

note eta: capital like English H - eitch
          small like English n - en

then we have some diphthongs
(letter combinations with unique sounds)
that are pronounced in exactly the same
way. ee as in _fee_. They are:

EI , ει   and   OI , oi'
unless the second letter is accented
which tends to separate their sound.
Confused? What did you expect
it _is_ Greek after all. NEXT PAGE.
The whole alphabet coming right up:

1 ALPHA   A , α   ALWAYS PRONOUNCED THE SAME - THANK GOD AS IN F<u>A</u>THER - HUT

2 BETA   B β   SAME AS THE ENGLISH V AS IN V<u>I</u>CTOR
vééta

3 GAMMA   Γ , γ   AS IN <u>Y</u>ES BUT BETTER ASK A GREEK AND PRACTICE A LOT

4 DELTA   Δ , δ   TH AS IN <u>TH</u>IS , <u>TH</u>AT
Thelta

5 EPSILON   E , ε   ALWAYS THE <u>E</u> AS IN <u>E</u>V<u>E</u>R N<u>E</u>V<u>E</u>R

6 ZETA
zeé ta

Z, j, z, ⊚ SURPRISE! BET YOU THOUGHT IT WAS THE LAST ONE! NOT IN GREEK. AS IN <u>Z</u>EST or <u>Z</u>EAL

7 ETA
eé ta

H, n ⊚ EE AS IN F<u>EE</u> or TR<u>EE</u>

8 THETA

θ, ϑ ⊚ <u>TH</u> SOUND BUT THIS TIME AS IN <u>TH</u>OUGHT or <u>TH</u>ESIS (which means seat in Greek, but that is another matter.)

9 IOTA
yo´ ta

I, i ⊚ REMEMBER? ALWAYS <u>EE</u> AS IN F<u>EE</u>. JUST A TAD SHORTER

16

10 KAPPA K u k ⊚ AN EASY ONE. JUST LIKE THE
ENGLISH K in <u>K</u>EY or <u>K</u>ITE
BUT NOT IN <u>K</u>NIFE

11 LAMDA Λ , λ ⊚ ALSO EASY L AS IN
<u>L</u>OOT or <u>L</u>OAF

12 MÉE M μ ⊚ THIS IS GETTING TO BE A SNAP.
EXACTLY AS IN <u>M</u>OTHER

13 NÉE N , ν ⊚ WE ARE ON A ROLL NOW! AS IN
<u>N</u>EW or <u>N</u>OW. CAREFUL, THE
SMALL NÉE LOOKS LIKE A VÉE ν

14 KSÉE Ξ , ʒ ⊚ OUR LUCK HAS ENDED. THIS HAS
THE KS - SOUND AS IN XERO<u>X</u>
OR E<u>XX</u>ON - E<u>X</u>IT

17

15 OMICRON O o 🌀   FOR EVER AND EVER O AS IN
                           BALL , FALL , CALL

16 PÉE Π, π 🌀   LUCKY AGAIN ! ENGLISH P
    sometimes fo   AS IN PEST - POSTER

17 RHO P p 🌀   AND ALL THIS TIME YOU THOUGHT
                           IT WAS P as in PEST. WELL IN
                           GREEK IT IS AN R* A ROLLED
                           ONE AT THAT AS IN RIVER
                           PRONOUNCED BY A MEXICAN

18 SIGMA Σ, σ 🌀   JUST LIKE THE S IN
    final s   SEEM OR SEAM

19 TUF T, τ THE ENGLISH T IS EXACTLY THE SAME $\underline{T}$IMBER

20 EÉPSILON Y, υ $\underline{\underline{EE}}$ AS IN F$\underline{\underline{EE}}$. JUST LIKE ETA (H, η) AND IOTA (I, ι)

21 PHÉE Φ, φ THE F OR PH SOUND $\underline{PH}$OTOGRA$\underline{\underline{PH}}$ − $\underline{\underline{F}}$IGHT BETTER ASK A GREEK HERE AS WELL.

22 HÉE X, χ

23 PSÉE $\Psi, \psi,$ AS IN $\underline{\underline{P}}$SYCHOLOGY OR PSEUDONYM PRONOUNCED BY A SCOTT

24 OMEGA Ω, ω FINALLY! EXACTLY LIKE OMICRON−JUST TO CONFUSE.

ONE LAST THING BUT ALL-IMPORTANT ARE
　　　more **DIPHTHONGS**
THERE ARE 2 DIPHTHONGS IN THE WORD DIPHTHONGS
ARE YOU LISPING?

AI - αι　alpha-iota　the E sound as in N<u>E</u>V<u>E</u>R

AY - αυ　alpha-eepsilon　the AV sound as in H<u>AV</u>E

EY - ευ } epsilon-eepsilon the EV sound as in <u>EV</u>ITA
　　　　　　　　　or EF　"　"　" L<u>EF</u>T

THERE JUST MAY BE A FEW MORE WHICH I MAY
HAVE FORGOTTEN. IF I FORGOT THEM THOUGH
MOST LIKELY YOU DON'T NEED THEM.

ACCENTS - PUNCTUATION MARKS
ASPIRATION MARKS AND THE LIKE

OF COURSE THERE ARE SOME OF THOSE, WHICH
IN RECENT YEARS HAVE BEEN SOMEWHAT SIMPLIFIED
- IT WAS ABOUT TIME - SUFFICE TO SAY THAT THE
GREEK QUESTION MARK ; IS THE SAME AS
THE SEMI-COLON OR IS IT THE COLON?

! / \ ~ ⊃ ⊂ . . « » ῀
· ( ) . . ⌐ ⌐ — / (STOP)

SAMPLES

MAIN PART

- SAYINGS - ADAGES
- WITTY REMARKS
- NOT SO WITTY REMARKS
- And other pedestrian and trite bits.

FORMAT

THE ENSUING PAGES WILL FOLLOW — MOST OF THE TIME — THE FORMAT BELOW

1   GREEK PHRASE IN CAPITALS

2   PRONUNCIATION IN ENGLISH

3   LITERAL TRANSLATION (FOR FUN)

4   MEANING & EQUIVALENT EXPRESSION
         (IF ONE EXISTS)

5   APPROPRIATE USAGE
         (IF WE FEEL LIKE IT)

*   There may be some illustrations
         (If we can think of any)

25

TPABAEI TA MANIA TOY

TRAVÁEE TA MALLÁ TOO

HE IS PULLING HIS HAIR

- HE IS AT WIT'S END

- HE IS DESPERATE

- HE DOESN'T KNOW WHAT
  TO DO SO WHY NOT?

- HE IS AT A LOOSE END

ΠΕΡΑΣΕ Η ΜΠΟΓΙΑ ΤΗΣ

PÉRASE EE BOYIÁ TIS

HER PAINT HAS PASSED

 SHE HAS SEEN BETTER DAYS

 SHE IS OVER THE HILL

ΕΚΑΝΕ ΤΑ ΣΤΡΑΒΑ ΜΑΤΙΑ

ÉKANE TA STRAVÁ MÁTIA

HE MADE CROOKED EYES

ΣTRAVA = CROOKED or BLIND

◎ HE TURNED A BLIND EYE

◉ HE PRETENDED NOT TO SEE

ΤΟΥΣ ΕΒΑΛΕ ΤΑ ΓΥΑΛΙΑ

toús évale ta yialiá

HE PUT ^{EYE} GLASSES ON THEM

⊚ — HE MADE THEM SEE WHAT THEY COULDN'T FOR THEMSELVES

⊚ — HE SHOWED THEM HOW TO DO SOMETHING THAT THEY COULD NOT FIGURE OUT HOW TO DO

ΠΙΑΝΕΙ ΠΟΥΛΙΑ ΣΤΟΝ ΑΕΡΑ

PIÁNI POOLIA STON AÉRA

HE CATCHES BIRDS
IN THE AIR (OUT OF
THE SKY)

◎ HE/SHE IS VERY SMART *

◎ HE IS AS SHARP AS A RAZOR

* Not used frequently.

31

TOY ΒΓΗΚΕ ΞΥΝΟ

TOO VGEÉKE KSEENÓ

IT CAME OUT SOUR FOR HIM

SPOILED THE FUN

UNFORTUNATE TURN OF EVENTS

ΚΑΒΑΛΗΣΕ ΤΟ ΚΑΛΑΜΙ

CAVÁLEESE TO CALÁMI

HE MOUNTED THE BAMBOO

◎ HE IS TOO BIG FOR HIS BOOTS
◎ HE THINKS HIGHLY OF HIMSELF

ΠΗΡΑΝ ΑΕΡΑ ΤΑ ΜΥΑΛΑ ΤΟΥ

PEÉRAN AÉRA TA MEEALÁ TOO

HIS BRAINS TOOK AIRS

⊚ HE HAS GROWN TOO BIG FOR HIS BOOTS
⊚ HE THINKS HIS S--T DOESN'T STINK (AMER.)
(sorry)

ΕΙΝΑΙ ΤΟΥ ΔΙΑΟΛΟΥ ΚΑΛΤΣΑ

EÉNE TOO THIAÓLOU KALTSA

HE IS DEVILS SOCKS
SHE-IT

HE IS CRAFTY, SLY, FOXY, CUNNING
EVEN DECEITFUL AND MAYBE SMART

ΕΓΙΝΕ ΚΑΠΝΟΣ

ÉGEENE KAPNÓS

HE BECAME SMOKE

HE DISAPPEARED QUICKLY

HE TOOK OFF LIKE A BAT OUT OF HELL

ΕΙΝΑΙ ΞΥΛΟ ΑΠΕΛΕΚΗΤΟ

ΕΕΝΕ KSEELO APELEKEETO

HE/SHE IS AN UNHEWN PIECE OF WOOD

◎ HE/SHE IS VULGAR - GROSS

◎ HE/SHE IS HIGHLY··· UNEDUCATED

*NOTE   ΕΙΝΑΙ = EENE = HE-SHE-IT IS
         ΕΙΣΑΙ = YOU ARE = EESE

ΤΑ ΦΟΡΤΩΣΕ ΣΤΟΝ ΚΟΚΚΟΡΑ

TA FÓRTOSE STON CÓCORA

HE LOADED THEM ON THE ROOSTER

◎ HE GAVE UP*
◎ HE RESIGNED FROM THE PURSUIT OF HIS GOAL

*SORT OF IMPLIES THAT HE IS DOING NOTHING NOW.

38

TOY ΕΒΑΛΕ ΤΑ ΔΥΟ ΠΟΔΙΑ Σ᾽ΕΝΑ ΠΑΠΟΥΤΣΙ

TO ÉVALE TA THIÓ PÓTHIA SÉNA PAPOÓTSI

SHE PUT HIS TWO FEET IN ONE SHOE

- SHE PUT HIM THROUGH THE MILL
- SHE IMPOSED HER WILL ON HIM
- SHE WEARS THE PANTS IN THE FAMILY
- SHE STRAIGHTENED HIM OUT
- SHE RULES THE ROOST
  (ALL OF THE ABOVE)

39

TOY ΑΛΛΑΞΕ ΤΑ ΦΩΤΑ

TOO ÁLAKSE TA FÓTA

HE CHANGED HIS LIGHTS

◎ HE TOOK ADVANTAGE OF HIM

◉ HE BEAT HIM BADLY

* MAS ÁLAKSES TA FÓTA : TO YOUR TROLLEY-BUS
DRIVER IN STOP & GO TRAFFIC.

40

MOY ΕΠΡΙΞΕΣ ΤΟ ΣΥΚΩΤΙ
MOO ÉPRIKSES TO SIKÓTEE

YOU MADE MY LIVER SWELL

YOU MADE ME SICK
YOU MAKE ME SICK

41

ΤΟΥ ΕΒΓΑΛΕ ΤΟ ΑΧΤΙ

ΤΟΟ ÉVGALE TO ÁCHTEE

HE TOOK MY ÁCHTEE* (*SPITE or GRUDGE?)

◎ HE WORKED ME TO DEATH
◎ HE MADE MY LIFE MISERABLE

42

TOY EKANE THN ZΩH ΠATINI

TOO ÉKANE TIN ZOÉE PATEÉNI

SHE MADE HIS LIFE A ROLLER SKATE
(sometimes also ΠOΔHΛATO = BICYCLE
    instead of roller scate. Don't ask why.)

SHE MADE HIS LIFE MISERABLE.

ZΩH = ΠATINI

* Also appropriate for mother-in-laws
  Or is it mothers-in-law?

ΤΟΥ ΤΑ ΕΨΑΛΕ

ΤΟΟ ΤΑ ÉPSALE

HE SANG PSALMS TO HIM

ⓐ HE TOLD HIM OFF

ⓑ HE CALLED HIM ON THE CARPET

ⓒ HE DRESSED HIM DOWN

TOY EBΓAΛE THN ΠIΣTH

TOO ÉVGALE TIN PÍSTEE

HE TOOK HIS FAITH OUT OF HIM

HE MADE HIS
LIFE MISERABLE *

* TO YOUR WAITER AFTER THE

FIRST HOUR OF WAITING.
/ MOO EVGALES .....

ΤΟΥ ΨΗΣΕ ΤΟ ΨΑΡΙ ΣΤΑ ΧΕΙΛΙΑ

TOÓPSEESE TO PSÁPI STA HEÉLIA

SHE COOKED THE FISH ON HIS LIPS

◎ SHE MADE HIS LIFE MISERABLE

◎ SHE NAGGED HIM TO DEATH

◎ SHE PUT HIM THROUGH THE MILL

46

ΕΓΙΝΕ ΠΥΡ ΚΑΙ ΜΑΝΙΑ

ÉGEENE PIR KAI MANÍA

HE BECAME FIRE AND MANIA

- HE SAW RED
- HE FLEW OFF THE HANDLE
- HE BLEW HIS TOP
- HE GOT VERY ANGRY
- HE'S MAD LIKE HELL

ΕΓΙΝΑΝ ΜΑΛΙΑ-ΚΟΥΒΑΡΙΑ

EGEENAN MALIÁ-KOOVARIA

THEY BECAME YARN AND SKEINS

(sometimes SPOOLS)

THEY CUT EACH OTHERS' THROATS

THEY GOT INTO A FIGHT

TA EKANAN ΓΥΑΛΙΑ-ΚΑΡΦΙΑ

TA ÉKANAN YALIÁ-KARFIÁ

THEY MADE THEM GLASSES-NAILS

◎ THEY WRECKED THE PLACE

◎ THEY TURNED IT UPSIDE DOWN

49

ΤΟΝ ΕΓΡΑΨΕ ΣΤΑ ΠΑΛΙΑ ΤΟΥ ΤΑ ΠΑΠΟΥΤΣΙΑ

TON ÉGRAPSE STA PALIÁ TOO TA PAPOÓTSIA

HE WROTE HIM IN/ON HIS OLD SHOES

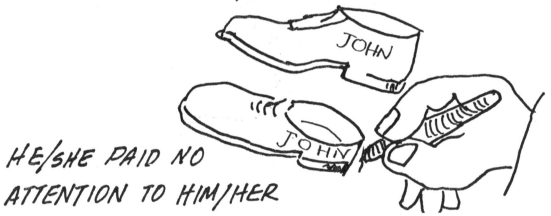

HE/SHE PAID NO
ATTENTION TO HIM/HER

* The feeling one usually gets in a restaurant or standing in some line.

50

ΘΑ ΦΑΝΕ ΤΑ ΜΟΥΣΤΑΚΙΑ ΤΟΥΣ

THA FÁNE TA MOOSTÁKIA TOOS

THEY WILL EAT THEIR MUSTACHES

THERE WILL BE A FREE-FOR-ALL

ΤΟΒΑΛΕ ΣΤΑ ΠΟΔΙΑ

ΤΌVALE STA PÓTHIA

HE PUT IT IN HIS FEET * OR LEGS
(ON)

TO   IT

HE TOOK OFF LIKE A BAT OUT OF HELL

* Feet and legs are the same word in Greek.

TOY ΠΗΡΕ ΤΟΝ ΑΕΡΑ

TOO PEÉRE TON AÉRA

HE TOOK HIS AIR

HE BECAME ^ FAMILIAR WITH HIM
        overly

ΔΕΝ ΞΕΡΟΥΝ ΠΟΥ ΠΑΝ ΤΑ ΤΕΣΣΕΡΑ

THEN KSÉROON POO PUN TA TÉSERA

THEY DON'T KNOW WHERE THE FOUR

ARE GOING

THEY ARE IGNORANT (UNTRAINED)

(they are untrained because they
can not be trained)

THEY DON'T KNOW IF THEY ARE COMING
OR GOING.

ΒΑΛΕ ΝΕΡΟ ΣΤΟ ΚΡΑΣΙ

VÁLE NERÓ STO KRASÍ

PUT SOME WATER IN THE WINE

URGING SOMEONE TO COMPROMISE*

* Good luck.

ΠΑΕΙ ΦΙΡΙ-ΦΙΡΙ

PÁEE FIRÍ-FIRÍ (FEEREÉ)
(pie)
HE IS GOING FIRÍ-FIRÍ*

HE IS ASKING FOR IT

* The word(s) FIRI-FIRI does NOT appear in any reference book nor does anyone know what it means. They use it anyway.

56

ΕΠΙΑΣΕ ΤΟΝ ΤΑΥΡΟ ΑΠΟ ΤΑ ΚΕΡΑΤΑ

ΕΡΙΑΣΕ ΤΟΝ ΤΑVΡΟ ΑΡΟ ΤΑ ΚΕΡΑΤΑ

HE TOOK THE BULL BY THE HORNS.

FOR THOSE WHO MAY NOT KNOW THIS.... METAPHOR:
HE IS IN CONTROL OF THINGS.

ΕΧΟΥΝΕ ΔΟΥΛΙΕΣ ΜΕ ΦΟΥΝΤΕΣ

ÉHOONE THOOLIÉS ME FOÓNDES

THEY HAVE BUSINESS WITH POM-POMS

◎ THEY HAVE A LOT OF BUSINESS
◎ THEY ARE DOING A BANG·UP BUSINESS (amer.)

58

TA ZOA MOY APΓA

TA ZÓA MOO ARGÁ

MY ANIMALS ARE SLOW

THIS ALSO IS USED TO DESCRIBE
SOMEONE WHO IS DOING SOMETHING
SLOWLY, BUT IT IMPLIES THAT HE/SHE
CAN NOT HELP IT.... BECAUSE OF
MENTAL-FUNCTION DIFFICULTIES.

TI KANEI NIAOY-NIAOY ΣTA KEPAMYΔIA;

TEÉ KÁNEE NIÁOO-NIÁOO STA KERAMÍTHIA ?

WHAT GOES MIEAW-MIEAW ON THE ROOF TOP?

WHEN STATING THE OBVIOUS
ISN'T IT OBVIOUS ?

ΓΛΕΝΤΙ ΤΡΙΚΟΥΒΕΡΤΟ

GLÉNDI TRICOÚVERTO

THREE - BLANKET PARTY

- ◎ A BALL
- ◎ BIG BASH - LOTS OF FUN - A BLAST.
- ◎ PARTY WITH EATING, DRINKING DANCING AND CAROUSING
- ◎ RAISED THE ROOF

ΜΠΗΚΕ ΤΟ ΝΕΡΟ ΣΤ᾽ΑΥΛΑΚΙ

BEÉKE TO NERÓ STAVLÁKEE

THE WATER GOT IN THE WATER DITCH

ⓢ THINGS GOT UNDER WAY - TOOK

THEIR NATURAL COURSE.
ⓢ STARTED THE BALL ROLLING

MAZI MIΛAME , XΩPIA KATAΛABAINOYME

MAZEÉ MILÁME, HÓRIA KATALAVÉNOUME

TOGETHER WE TALK, SEPARATELY WE
UNDERSTAND

⊚ WE ARE NOT COMMUNICATING

⊚ YOU DON'T SEEM TO UNDERSTAND ME

⊚ WE DON'T SPEAK THE SAME LANGUAGE

ΚΑΘΕ ΕΜΠΟΔΙΟ ΓΙΑ ΚΑΛΟ

KÁTHE EMBÓTHIO YA KALÓ

EVERY HURDLE FOR THE BEST
(OBSTACLE)

⊚ EVERYTHING IS FOR THE BEST

⊚ USED TO RATIONALIZE FAILURE

ΥΠΟΣΧΕΤΑΙ ΛΑΓΟΥΣ ΜΕ ΠΕΤΡΑΧΕΙΛΙΑ

EEPÓS-HETE LAGOÓS ME PETRAHEÉLIA

HE PROMISES RABBITS WITH CLERIC'S STOLE

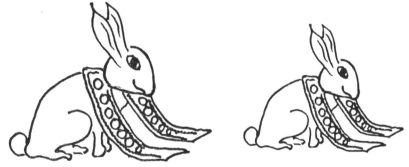

HE PROMISES THE SUN AND THE MOON
OR THE EARTH AND THE MOON, IF YOU WISH.

GREEK POLITICIANS DO. SADLY GREEKS
BELIEVE THEM. THE SUN AND MOON ARE STILL THERE.

ΕΧΑΣΕ ΤΟΝ ΜΠΟΥΣΟΥΛΑ

ÉHASE TON BOÓSOOLA

HE LOST THE COMPASS

◎ HE HAS LOST HIS DIRECTION

◎ HE IS CONFUSED - MIXED UP

ΑΥΤΟΣ ΑΓΡΟΝ ΗΓΟΡΑΖΕ

AFTÓS AGRÓN EEGÓRAZE

HE WAS BUYING A FARM
(FIELD)

◎ HE COULDN'T CARE LESS

◎ HE WAS INATTENTIVE

TO ΦΥΣΑΕΙ ΚΑΙ ΔΕΝ ΚΡΥΩΝΕΙ

TO FEESÁEE KÉ THEN KREEÓNEE

HE BLOWS ON IT BUT IT DOESN'T COOL OFF

◎ HE DUG HIS OWN GRAVE
◎ NOTHING HE CAN DO MAKES HIM FEEL BETTER
◎ HE CAN DO NOTHING TO CORRECT PAST MISTAKES
◎ HE IS RIGHTFULLY SUFFERING FROM PAST ERRORS
AND MISJUDGEMENTS.

BANE MYANO

VÁLE MIALÓ

PUT SOME BRAINS IN

BE SENSIBLE

IT IS OFTEN USED IN VARIOUS FORMS
AND ALL THE TENSES

XTIZEI ΠAΛATIA ΣTHN AMMO

HTEÉZEE PALÁTIA STÍN ĀMO

HE IS BUILDING PALACES IN THE SAND

BUILDING CASTLES IN THE AIR

TAZEI TON OYPANO ME T'AΣTPA

TÁZEE TON OORANÓ ME TÁSTRA

HE PROMISES THE SKY WITH ITS STARS

HE PROMISES THE EARTH AND THE MOON

ΕΤΕΡΟΝ - ΕΚΑΤΕΡΟΝ

ÉTERON - EKÁTERON

ONE THING - ANOTHER THING

◎ THERE ARE TWO ENTIRELY DIFFERENT MATTERS

◎ IT'S A HORSE OF A DIFFERENT COLOR

◎ LIKE COMPARING APPLES AND ORANGES

ΔEN KANOYN XΩPIO

THEN KÁNOON HORIÓ

THEY DON'T MAKE A VILLAGE

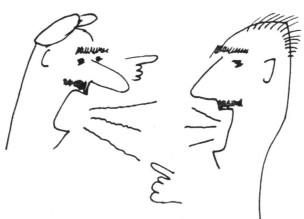

◎ THEY DON'T GET ALONG
◎ THEY DON'T SEE EYE TO EYE

TÁKA - TÁKA

TAKA - TAKA

TAKA - TAKA (NO TRANSLATION.
NO ONE KNOWS JUST
WHAT IT MEANS)

(and sometimes TSÁKA-
TSÁKA.

🌀 VERY QUICKLY

🌀 WITH LIGHTNING SPEED *

* An extremely rare occurence in Greece.

74

ΣΤΟ ΑΨΕ-ΣΒΗΣΕ

STO APSE-SVEÉSE

AT THE ON-OFF

IN NO TIME AT ALL*

* In Greece anything that takes less than 100 years.

ΣΤΟ ΠΙ ΚΑΙ ΦΙ

STO PEÉ KE FEE

IN PI AND PHI

◎ IMMEDIATELY! IF NOT SOONER

◎ RIGHT NOW.

◎ WHEN SOMETHING IS DONE QUICKLY &
EFFKIENTLY *

* which is seldom

AN ΣΠΑΣΕΙ Ο ΔΙΑΒΟΛΟΣ ΤΟ ΠΟΔΑΡΙ ΤΟΥ

AN SPÁSEE O THIÁVOLOS TO POTHÁRI TOO

IF THE DEVIL BREAKS HIS LEG

IF WORSE COMES TO WORSE

ΚΑΤΟΠΙΝ ΕΟΡΤΗΣ

CATÓPIN EORTÍS

AFTER THE HOLIDAY

AFTER THE FACT

ΜΠΡΟΣ ΓΚΡΕΜΟΣ ΚΑΙ ΠΙΣΩ ΡΕΜΑ

BROS GREMÓS KÉ PEÉSO RÉMA

CLIFF AHEAD AND RAVINE BEHIND

BETWEEN THE DEVIL AND
THE DEEP BLUE SEA.

ΕΦΤΑΣΕ Ο ΚΟΜΠΟΣ ΣΤΟ ΧΤΕΝΙ

ÉFTASE Ο CÓMBOS STO HTÉNI

THE KNOT REACHED THE COMB

DECISION TIME . THE EQUIVALENT,
IN A WAY, OF THE GREAT AMERICAN
ADAGE "S--T OR GET OFF THE POT "

TA PAΣA ΔEN KANOYN TON ΠAΠA

TA RÁSA THEN KÁNOON TON PAPÁ

THE VESTMENTS DON'T MAKE
                    THE PRIEST

JUST BECAUSE ONE MAY BE WELL QUALIFIED
ON PAPER THAT DOES NOT MAKE HIM/HER
GOOD IN PRACTICE.

81

ΓΙΑ ΨΥΛΛΟΥ ΠΗΔΗΜΑ

YA PSEÉLOO PEÉTHEEMA

FOR A FLEA'S JUMP

FOR NO REASON AT ALL

ΤΙ ΤΡΕΧΕΙ;

TEE TRÉHEE;?

WHAT'S RUNNING?

◉ WHAT'S HAPPENING?

◉ WHAT'S GOING ON?

◉ WHAT'S COOKING?

ΕΙΠΕ Ο ΓΑΪΔΑΡΟΣ ΤΟΝ ΠΕΤΕΙΝΟ ΚΕΦΑΛΑ

ΕΕΡΕ Ο GÁÏTHAROS ΤΟΝ PETINÓ KEFÁLA

THE DONKEY CALLED THE ROOSTER BIGHEAD

(FATHEAD)

LOOK WHO'S CALLING THE KETTLE BLACK!

84

ΣΤΗΝ ΒΡΑΣΗ ΚΟΛΑΕΙ ΤΟ ΣΙΔΕΡΟ

STIN VRÁSEE KOLÁEE TÓ SITHERO

THE IRON STICKS WHEN ITS HOT

 — NOW IS THE BEST TIME — IT'S NOW OR NEVER

 — THE BEST TIME TO DO SOMETHING IS WHEN THINGS ARE HOT.

 — STRIKE WHEN THE IRON IS HOT.

ΚΑΛΗΜΕΡΑ ΓΙ'ΑΥΡΙΟ

KALIMÉRA YIÁVRIO

GOOD MORNING FOR TOMORROW

IT IS USED TO DESCRIBE SOMEONE WHO
IS PERFORMING A TASK TOO SLOWLY

ΤΡΑΒΑΕΙ ΚΟΥΠΙ

TRAVÁEE KOOPEÉ

HE IS ROWING (PULLING AN OAR)

- HE TOES THE LINE
- HE IS WORKING HARD - CARRYING THE BURDEN (SELDOM USED!!)

ΑΡΤΖΙ-ΜΠΟΥΡΤΖΙ ΚΑΙ ΛΟΥΛΑΣ

ÁRDGEE - BÓORDGEE KE LOOLÁS

(NO POSSIBLE TRANSLATION -THESE
WORDS EXIST NOWHERE ELSE - BUT
SOUND FUNNY ANYWAY)

◎ IT EXPRESSES INCOHERENCE AND
ABSURDITY AND A CONFUSED STATE
WHICH IS WHY IT IS USED EXTENSIVELY!

◎ GOBBLE-DY-GOOK ?

ΜΕ ΔΟΥΛΕΥΕΙΣ;
MÉ THOOLÉVIS?

ARE YOU WORKING ME?

 ARE YOU KIDDING ME?
 ARE YOU SERIOUS? YOU CAN'T BE SERIOUS?!

ΣΕ ΔΟΥΛΕΥΟ -
SE THOOLÉVO = I AM JUST KIDDING YOU

OYTE ΨΥΛΛΟΣ ΣΤΟΝ ΚΟΡΦΟ ΣΟΥ

OÓTE PSEÉLOS STON KÓRFO SOO

NOT A FLEA IN YOUR BOSOM.

SOMETHING TO BE AVOIDED AT
ALL COSTS. USED AS AN APHORISM.

MOY ΖHKΩΘHKE H TPIXA

MOO SICÓTHIKE EE TREÉHA

MY HAIR WAS RAISED

I WAS APPALLED

NOW YOU KNOW WHY SOME GREEKS
ALBEIT A FEW, TOO FEW, WALK AROUND
WITH RAISED HAIR

ΠΟΙΟΣ ΘΑ ΒΓΑΛΕΙ ΤΟ ΦΙΔΙ ΑΠΟ ΤΗΝ ΤΡΥΠΑ;

PIÓS THÁ VGÁLEE TO FÍTHEE APÓ TIN TREÉPA;?

WHO'S GOING TO GET THE SNAKE OUT OF THE HOLE?

◎ WHO'S GOING TO TAKE CHARGE?

◎ WHO"LL DO THE NASTY JOB?

ΜΑΣ ΦΩΤΙΣΕΣ!

MAS FÓTISES!

YOU TURNED ON OUR LIGHT

SARCASTICALLY : YOU WERE VERY INFORMATIVE MEANING (A) YOU SAID THE OBVIOUS (B) WHAT YOU SAID WAS AS CLEAR AS MUD AND MAKES ABSOLUTELY NO SENSE.

ΜΟΥΡΘΕ Ο ΟΥΡΑΝΟΣ ΣΦΟΝΤΥΛΙ

MOÓRTHE O OÓRANOS SFONDÉELEE

THE SKY HIT ME LIKE A SPINDLE

◎ I WAS TAKEN BY SURPRISE - I WAS HIT HARD
◉ I WAS FLABBERGASTED!

NA MOY TPYΠHΣEIΣ THN MYTH

NA MOO TREEPEÉSIS TIN MEÉTI

MAKE A HOLE IN MY NOSE

◎ I CAN'T BELIEVE IT
◎ I'LL EAT MY HAT
◎ I HAVE TO SEE IT TO
BELIEVE IT

Μ'ΕΒΓΑΛΕ ΑΣΠΡΟΠΡΟΣΩΠΟ

MÉVGALE ASPROPRÓSOPO

HE GOT ME OUT WHITEFACED

◉ HE SERVED ME WELL

◉ HE PROVED ME RIGHT

◉ HE IS A SOURCE OF PRIDE FOR ME

MOU ΠΕΣΑΝΕ ΤΑ ΜΟΥΤΡΑ

MOO PÉSANE TA MOOTRA

MY FACE DROPPED

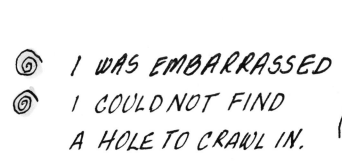
I WAS EMBARRASSED
I COULD NOT FIND
A HOLE TO CRAWL IN.

ΔΕΝ ΤΑ ΒΓΑΖΕΙ ΠΕΡΑ

THEN TA VGÁZEE PÉRA

HE DOESN'T TAKE IT OUT THERE

⊚ HE CAN'T MANAGE

⊚ HE CAN'T MAKE ENDS MEET

ΕΚΑΝΕ ΜΙΑ ΤΡΥΠΑ ΣΤΟ ΝΕΡΟ

ÉKANE MIÁ TREÉPA STO NERÓ

HE MADE A HOLE IN THE WATER

- HE WAS UNSUCCESSFUL - HE FAILED
- HIS EFFORTS MEANT NOTHING
- LOTS OF WORK - NO RESULTS

ΑΠ᾽ΕΞΩ ΚΑΙ ΑΝΑΚΑΤΩΤΑ

ΑΡΈΚSO ΚΕ ΑΝΑΚΑΤΟΤΆ

FROM THE OUTSIDE AND ALL MIXED UP

◎ TO KNOW SOMETHING INSIDE-OUT

◎ TO KNOW SOMETHING LIKE THE
BACK OF YOUR HAND

◎ TO KNOW SOMETHING BY HEART

ΚΑΛΑ ΝΑ ΠΑΘΕΙ

KALÁ NA PÁTHEE

WELL HE SUFFERED (SORRY)

IT SERVES HIM RIGHT

HE SUFFERS BECAUSE OF HIS OWN
DOING - HE DESERVES WHAT HE GETS

ΕΓΙΝΕ ΤΥΦΛΑ ΣΤΟ ΜΕΘΥΣΙ

ÉGINE TEÉFLA STO METHEÉSEE

HE BECAME BLINDLY DRUNK

HE WAS AS DRUNK AS A SKUNK

HE WAS SLOSHED

ΔΕΝ ΙΔΡΩΝΕΙ ΤΟ ΑΦΤΙ ΤΟΥ

THEN EETHRÓNEE TO AFTEÉ TOO

HIS EAR DOES NOT SWEAT

◎ HE TURNS A DEAF EAR

◎ HE LISTENS TO NO ONE BUT HIMSELF *

* Not an unusual phenomenon in Greece.

ΦΥΡΔΗΝ - ΜΙΓΔΗΝ

FEÉRTHEEN - MEÉGTHEEN

(HAVEN'T THE SLIGHTEST IDEA
WHAT IT MEANS, BUT I DO LIKE
THE SOUND OF IT.)

◎ A MESS
◎ A MIXED·UP MESS
◎ (PELL)·PELL·MELL I MEANT

ΕΒΓΑΛΕ ΓΛΩΣΣΑ

ÉVGALE GLÓSSA

HE/SHE STUCK HER TONGUE OUT

◎ HE SASSED (WAS DISRESPECTFUL)

◎ HE TALKED BACK

◎ HE MOUTHED-OFF (Amer.)

ΟΤΙ ΒΡΕΞΕΙ ΑΣ ΚΑΤΕΒΑΣΕΙ

ÓTEE VRÉKSI AS KATEVÁSI

WHATEVER IT RAINS, LET IT COME DOWN

◎ WHATEVER HAPPENS, HAPPENS

◎ WHAT WILL BE, WILL BE (ALMOST)

ΔΑΓΚΩΣΕ ΤΗΝ ΛΑΜΑΡΙΝΑ

THÁNGOSE TIN LAMARINA

HE BIT THE SHEET METAL

⊚ HE WAS SMITTEN

⊚ HE FELL HEAD OVER HEELS
(IN LOVE)

ΒΡΕΧΕΙ ΚΑΡΕΚΛΟΠΟΔΑΡΑ

VRÉHEE CARECLOPÓTHARA
(FOR ADVANCED STUDENTS)

IT'S RAINING CHAIRLEGS

ΡΙΧΝΕΙ ΚΑΛΑΠΟΔΙΑ

RÍHNEE KALAPODIA

IT'S POURING LASTS
(SHOE·LASTS *)

IT'S RAINING CATS AND DOGS

(and you thought Greek was peculiar?)

* Wooden shoe forms.

108

ΤΟΥ ΚΡΑΤΑΕΙ ΜΟΥΤΡΑ

TOO CRATÁEE MOÓTRA

HE IS HOLDING FACES

◎ HE IS ANGRY AT HIM

◎ HE IS SNUBBING HIM

ΠΑΡΕ-ΔΟΣΕ

PÁRE-THOSE

TAKE - GIVE *

◎ HAVING DEALINGS WITH SOMEONE
◎ DOING BUSINESS

* Notice that even though it does not mean the same thing, the order in English is reversed GIVE & TAKE.

ΑΥΤΟΣ, ΤΟ ΒΙΟΛΙ ΤΟΥ

AFTÓS TO VIOLÍ TOU

HE KEEPS ON PLAYING HIS VIOLIN

TO EXPRESS INSISTENCE OR EVEN SOMETIMES PERSISTENCE. OTHERS MAY BE TALKING OR BOTHERING HIM BUT HE KEEPS ON DOING HIS OWN THING.

ΚΥΛΙΣΕ Ο ΤΕΤΖΕΡΙΣ ΚΑΙ ΒΡΗΚΕ ΤΟ ΚΑΠΑΚΙ

KEÉLEESE O TÉTZERIS KÉ VREÉKE TO KAPAKI

THE POT ROLLED AND FOUND THE LID

YOU FOUND YOUR MATCH - HE FOUND HIS E.T.C.

TOY ΚΟΣΤΙΣΕ Ο ΚΟΥΚΟΣ ΑΗΔΟΝΙ

TOO CÓSTEESE O COÓKOS E I THÓNI

HE PAID THE PRICE OF A NIGHTINGALE
FOR A CUCKOO BIRD.

HE PAID THROUGH THE NOSE
IT COST HIM AN ARM AND A LEG
(IT COST A LOT MORE THAN IT SHOULD HAVE)

ΜΠΗΤΕ ΣΚΥΛΟΙ ΑΛΕΣΤΕ....

BEÉTE SKEÉLEE ALÉSTE

GO IN DOGS AND MAKE FLOUR (MILL)

DO AS YOU PLEASE WITHOUT SUFFERING
ANY CONSEQUENCES

ΤΟ ΠΛΗΡΩΣΕ ΜΕ ΤΑ ΜΑΛΙΑ ΤΗΣ ΚΕΦΑΛΗΣ ΤΟΥ

TO PLEÉROSE ME TA MALIÁ 'TIS KEFALÍS TOO

HE PAID FOR IT WITH THE HAIR ON HIS HEAD *

 IT COST AN ARM AND A LEG
 IT COST HIM A PRETTY PENNY

* That is why so many Greeks are bald or balding

ΠΛΗΡΩΣΕ ΤΗΝ ΝΥΦΗ

PLEÉROSE TIN NEÉFEE

HE PAID THE BRIDE

PAY THE PIPER

HE WAS BLAMED FOR WHAT HAPPENED
(whether he was at fault or not)*

* No one in Greece ever is or ever has been at fault for anything - and never will be!!
so the piper goes hungry.

116

ΕΙΝΑΙ ΑΝΩ ΠΟΤΑΜΩΝ

EÉNE ÁNO POTAMÓN

HE IS ABOVE/OVER RIVERS

◎ HE SEES RED

◎ BEYOND DESCRIPTION

◎ HE IS FIT TO BE TIED

◎ HE IS VERY-VERY ANGRY/MAD * **

* Have no idea what it has to do with rivers.
Frequently encountered in trolley buses, on boats, in the street and generally everywhere.

ΕΦΑΓΕ Η ΜΥΓΑ ΣΙΔΕΡΟ ΚΑΙ ΤΟ ΚΟΥΝΟΥΠΙ ΑΤΣΑΛΙ

ÉFAGE EE MEÉGA SÍTHERO KÉ TO KOONÓOPI ATSÁlEE

THE FLY ATE IRON AND THE MOSQUITO ATE STEEL

◎ THEY TURNED THE PLACE UPSIDE-DOWN

◎ THEY MADE A SHAMBLES OUT OF IT.

Great   or
◎ A ~~GOOD~~ TIME WAS HAD BY ALL.

118

ΔΕΝ ΧΑΡΙΖΕΙ ΚΑΣΤΑΝΑ

THEN HAREÉZEE KÁSTANA

HE DOESN'T GIVE CHESTNUTS AS GIFTS

- ◎ HE DRIVES A HARD BARGAIN
- ◎ HE IS HARD TO DEAL WITH
- ◎ HE IS UNFORGIVING
- ◎ THERE IS NO FREE LUNCH
- ◎ YOU CAN'T GET SOMETHING FOR NOTHING
- * something like that, or all of them.

119

ΖΗΣΕ ΜΑΙ ΜΟΥ ΝΑ ΦΑΣ ΤΡΙΦΥΛΛΙ

ZEÉSE MÝ MOO NA FÁS TRIFEÉLI

MAY YOU LIVE LONG ENOUGH MY MAY (month)
TO EAT THREE-LEAF CLOVER

SHOULD I LIVE TO SEE THE DAY

ΤΟΝ ΠΗΡΕ ΣΤΟΝ ΛΑΙΜΟ ΤΟΥ

TON PÉERE STON LEMÓ TOO

HE TOOK HIM ON HIS NECK

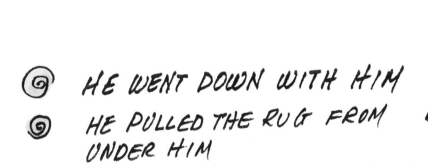

◎ HE WENT DOWN WITH HIM

◎ HE PULLED THE RUG FROM
UNDER HIM

ΔΕΝ ΕΙΝΑΙ ΠΑΙΞΕ-ΓΕΛΑΣΕ

THEN EÉNE PÉKSE-YÉLASE

IT ISN'T PLAY-LAUGH

NOT FUN & GAMES - IT IS A
SERIOUS MATTER OR A
DIFFICULT ONE.

TA EKANE ΘΑΛΑΣΣΑ

TA ÉKANE THÁLASA

HE MADE THEM SEA

HE MADE A MESS OF IT (again)

TA EKANE ΣΑΛΑΤΑ

TÁ ÉKANE   SALÁTA

HE MADE THEM SALAD

ⓢ HE MADE A MESS OF IT

ⓢ HE SCREWED-UP

TA EKANE MOYΣKEMA

TA ÉKANE MOOSKEMA

HE MADE THEM DRIPPING WET

HE MADE A MESS OF IT. (again)

* Amazing how many expressions there are about screwing up in Greece. I wonder why?

Η ΓΛΩΣΣΑ ΤΗΣ ΚΟΒΕΙ ΚΑΙ ΡΑΒΕΙ

EE GLÓSSA TIS KÓVEE KÉ RÁVEE

HER TONGUE CUTS AND SEWS

◎ SHE DOESN'T KNOW WHEN TO SHUT UP
◎ SHE IS A MOTORMOUTH

IT DOES IMPLY SHE IS A GOSSIP AS WELL

ΕΧΕ ΤΑ ΜΑΤΙΑ ΔΕΚΑΤΕΣΣΑΡΑ

EHE TA MÁTIA THEKATÉSSARA

HAVE YOUR EYES FOURTEEN

BE VERY CAREFUL

* A lesser warning is to have them just four-tessera.

ΕΞΩ ΚΟΥΚΛΑ - ΜΕΣΑ ΠΑΝΟΥΚΛΑ

EKSO KOÓKLA - MÉSA PANOÓKLA

OUTSIDE A DOLL - INSIDE THE PLAGUE

◎ YOU CAN'T JUDGE A BOOK BY ITS COVER

◎ THINGS AIN'T always WHAT THEY SEEM.

ΜΥΡΙΣΑ ΤΑ ΝΥΧΙΑ ΜΟΥ

MEÉREESA TA NEÉHIA MOO

I SMELLED MY FINGERNAILS

◎ WHEN YOU DO NOT WANT TO
DISCLOSE THE SOURCE OF
YOUR INFORMATION.
◎ A LITTLE BIRD TOLD ME

ΝΑ ΓΛΥΦΕΙΣ ΤΑ ΔΑΚΤΥΛΑ ΣΟΥ

NA GLEÉFIS TA THÁKTYLÁ SOO

TO LICK YOUR FINGERS

THE FOOD WAS SO GOOD
(A SUBTLE WAY OF SUGGESTING THAT PEOPLE
STILL EAT WITH THEIR FINGERS)

ΝΑ ΖΟΥ ΔΕΙΞΩ ΠΟΣΑ ΑΠΙΔΙΑ ΧΩΡΑΕΙ Ο ΣΑΚΟΣ

NA SOO THEÉKSO PÓSA APÍTHIA HORÁEE O SÁKOS

I''LL SHOW YOU HOW MANY APÍTHIA THE SACK HOLDS
Pears?

IT''LL GET WORSE BEFORE
IT''LL GET BETTER

ΕΧΩ ΤΟ ΠΑΝΩ ΧΕΡΙ

ÉHO TO PÁNO HÉRI

I HAVE THE UPPER HAND

I HAVE THE UPPER HAND

BET ALL THIS TIME YOU THOUGHT THE ONLY THING
COMMON IN THE TWO LANGUAGES WAS THE
WORD "DIPHTHONG"!

ΔΕΝ ΜΟΥ ΓΕΜΙΖΕΙ ΤΟ ΜΑΤΙ

THEN MOO YEMEÉZEE TO MÁTEE

HE
SHE } DOESN'T FILL MY EYE
IT

◎ I AM NOT IMPRESSED!
◎ IT CUTS NO ICE

133

MOY῾ΚΟΨΕ ΤΗΝ ΧΟΛΗ

MOÓ COPSE TIN HOLÉE

HE⎫
SHE⎬ SNAPPED MY GALL BLADER
IT⎭

◎ I WAS SCARED TO DEATH
(IF NOT THAT MUCH AT LEAST STUNNED)

◎ I WAS SCARED S--TLESS (sorry again)

NA MOY ΛΕΙΠΕΙ ΤΟ ΒΥΣΙΝΟ

NA MOO LEÉPEE TO VEÉSEENO

I CAN DO WITHOUT THE MARASCHINO
(CHERRY)

① I HAVE NO USE FOR IT
② I DON'T WANT IT

ΚΟΥΝΙΣΟΥ ΑΠ'ΤΗΝ ΘΕΣΗ ΣΟΥ

KOONEÉSOO AP TIN THÉSI SOO

MOVE FROM YOUR SEAT

THIS HAS GOT TO DO WITH PREJUDICES AND EVIL
SPIRITS. THE MERE THOUGHT OF SOMETHING, MAY
MAKE IT HAPPEN. IN A DISCUSSION, IF THE POSSIBILITY
OF THE WORSE THAT COULD HAPPEN IS DISASTROUS, THE
RESPONSE TO BREAK THE SPELL IS TO MOVE A BIT.

ΤΡΕΧΩ ΚΑΙ ΔΕΝ ΦΤΑΝΩ

TRÉHO KE THEN FTÁNO

I RUN AND CAN'T GET THERE

I CAN'T CATCH UP WITH ALL I GOT TO DO

ΟΤΙ ΕΧΩ ΚΑΙ ΔΕΝ ΕΧΩ

ÓTEE ÉHO KÉ THEN ÉHO

WHAT I HAVE AND DON'T HAVE

◎ ALL I'VE GOT - EVERYTHING
◎ LOCK, STOCK AND BARREL
◎ KIT AND KABOODLE, THE WHOLE 9 YARDS

ΔΕΝ ΧΑΛΑῼ ΤΗΝ ΖΑΧΑΡΕΝΙΑ ΜΟΥ

THEN HALÁO TIN ZAHARÉNIA MOO

1- I WON'T SPOIL MY SWEETNESS

2- I AM NOT SPOILING MY SUGARY

ⓢ I WON'T LOSE ANY SLEEP OVER IT

ⓢ IT AIN'T GONNA BOTHER ME NONE (amer.)

ΟΤΑΝ ΠΗΓΑΙΝΕΣ ΕΓΩ ΓΥΡΙΖΑ
ΌΤΑΝ PEÉGENES EGO GEÉRIZA

WHEN YOU WERE GOING I WAS RETURNING

THIS EXRESSES A PERSON'S GREATER
EXPERIENCE IN LIFE, AND CONSEQUENTLY
GREATER WISDOM

ΕΜΕΙΣ ΤΡΩΜΕ ΚΟΥΤΟΧΟΡΤΟ;

EMEÉS TRÓME KOUTÓHORTO?

ARE WE EATING IDIOT-WEEDS?

DO YOU THINK I AM STUPID?

WHAT DO YOU TAKE ME FOR?

ΑΣΤΑ ΒΡΑΣΤΑ

ÁSTA VRÁSTA

LET THEM BOIL

⊚ TO HECK WITH IT
⊚ A STATEMENT OF RESIGNATION

* This is a safe and benign enough expression. Use it liberally.

ΦΕΞΕ ΜΟΥ ΚΑΙ ΓΛΙΣΤΡΗΣΑ

FÉKSE MOO KÉ GLEÉSTRISA

LIGHT, ME AND I SLIPPED
(my way)

◎ EXPRESSES THE IMPROBABILITY
OF SOMETHING(s)   OCCURING
◎ I SHOULD LIVE LONG ENOUGH TO SEE IT!
◎ THE PIE IN THE SKY SYNDROM

I

ΚΑΝΑΜΕ ΠΛΑΚΑ

CÁNAME PLÁKA

WE MADE A TILE
     (CERAMIC)

II

ΣΠΑΣΑΜΕ ΠΛΑΚΑ

SPÁSAME PLAKA

WE BROKE A TILE
     (ALSO CERAMIC)

◎   WE HAD A LOT OF LAUGHS

◎   WE HAD A GOOD-FUN TIME

144

ΜΗΝ ΜΗΠΑΣ ΜΕΣΑ ΑΠ᾽ΤΑ ΔΟΝΤΙΑ ΣΟΥ

MEÉN MEELÁS MÉSA AP TA (TH)ĎONTIA SOO

DON'T SPEAK FROM INSIDE YOUR TEETH

DON'T BEAT AROUND THE BUSH
(or about)

ΚΟΛΟΚΥΘΙΑ ΜΕ ΡΙΓΑΝΗ

KOLOKEÉTHIA ME REÉGANI

ZUCHINI WITH OREGANO!!

PHOOEY! BALONEY! BULLSHIT! (pardon me)

* You may use it anywhere except in restaurants and tavernas. They d on't taste very well!

ΔΕΝ ΒΡΙΣΚΕΙΣ ΑΚΡΗ

THEN VREÉSKIS ÁKRI

YOU CAN'T FIND AN END

⊚ ALSO EXPRESSING FUTILITY AND
RESIGNATION.
⊚ YOU CAN'T FIND AN ANSWER
⊚ YOU CAN GET NO SATISFACTION (oops)

TPEXA - ΓΥΡΕΥΕ

TRÉXA - YEEREVE

RUN - SEARCH

◎ ALSO TO EXPRESS FUTILITY
AND RESIGNATION
◎ YOU CAN'T GET ANY STRAIGHT
ANSWERS

ΔΥΟ ΚΑΡΠΟΥΖΙΑ ΣΕ ΜΙΑ ΜΑΣΧΑΛΗ
ΔΕΝ ΧΩΡΑΝΕ

THIO KARPOÓZIA SE MIÁ MAS-HÁLI
THEN HORÁNE

TWO WATERMELON DON'T FIT
UNDER THE SAME ARM

YOU CAN'T SERVE TWO MASTERS AT THE SAME TIME

ΑΠΟ ΤΟ ΣΤΟΜΑ ΣΟΥ ΚΑΙ ΣΤΟΥ ΘΕΟΥ Τ'ΑΦΤΙ

APÓ TO STÓMA SOO KE STOO THEOÓ TAFTÉE

FROM YOUR MOUTH TO GOD'S EAR

MAY THE LORD HEAR YOU.

TΡΩΩ THN ΩΡA MOY

TRÓ-O TIN ÓRA MOO

I AM EATING MY TIME

G I AM KILLING TIME

I AM WASTING TIME

TRÓEE TIN ORA TOO = HE IS WASTING

HIS TIME

ΒΑΡΑΕΙ ΜΥΓΕΣ

VARÁEE MEÉYES

HE IS SWATTING FLIES

TO DESCRIBE SOMEONE WHO'S WASTING
TIME. E.g. CIVIL SERVANTS*

* *Warning*: Do not use in their presence. If you must, then whisper quietly.

ΓΥΡΕΥΕΙΣ ΨΥΛΛΟΥΣ ΣΤ'ΑΧΥΡΑ

YEERÉVIS PSEÉLOOS STA ÁHEERA

YOU ARE LOOKING FOR FLEAS IN A HAYSTACK

⊚ LIKE LOOKING FOR A NEEDLE IN A HAYSTACK

⊚ IN GREECE ALSO WHEN YOU ARE ASKING
FOR TOO MUCH DETAIL

ΤΗΣ ΚΥΡΙΑΚΗΣ ΧΑΡΑ ΚΑΙ ΤΗΣ ΔΕΥΤΕΡΑΣ ΛΥΠΗ

TIS KIRIAKIS HARÁ KÉ TIS THEFTÉRAS LEÉPI.

SUNDAY'S JOY - MONDAY'S SADNESS

THINK BEFORE YOU ACT

THINK BEFORE YOU LEAP

ΕΚΑΝΕ ΤΟΥ ΚΕΦΑΛΙΟΥ ΤΟΥ

ÉKANE TOU KEFALIOÚ TOO

HE DID OF HIS HEAD

HE DID AS HE PLEASED
(TAKING NO ONE INTO ACCOUNT)

ΟΧΙ ΓΙΑΝΝΗΣ, ΓΙΑΝΝΑΚΗΣ

OHI YÁNIS, YANNÁKIS

NOT JOHN, BUT JOHNY

① SIX OF ONE, HALF A DOZEN OF THE OTHER
② A ROSE BY ANY OTHER ~~COLOR~~ NAME . . . . .
③ THE SAME THING

156

ΣΑΝ ^{ΤΟ} ΨΑΡΙ ΣΤΗΝ ΣΤΕΡΙΑ

SUN ^{ΤΟ} ∧PSÁRI STEÉN STERIÁ

LIKE A FISH ON DRY LAND

LIKE A FISH OUT OF WATER

157

NETA - ΣKETA

NÉTA - SKÉTA.

NET - PLAIN

◎ PLAIN TALK
◎ THE BOTTOM LINE
◎ DON'T BEAT ABOUT THE BUSH.

ΕΒΑΛΕ ΦΕΣΙ

ÉVALE FÉSEE

HE PUT ON A FEZ

HE IS IN DEBT UP TO
HIS EARS (NECK?)

ΠΙΣΩ ΕΧΕΙ Η ΑΧΛΑΔΑ ΤΗΝ ΟΥΡΑ

PEÉSO ÉHEE AHLÁTHA TIN OORA

THE PEAR TREE HAS ITS TAIL BEHIND IT

◎ THERE IS MORE TO HIM/HER/IT
THAN IT'S SHOWING
◎ DESCRIBING SOMEONE WHO IS SLY-FOXY
◎ THERE IS MORE TO IT THAN MEETS THE EYE

KANEI THN ΠΑΠΙΑ

KÁNEE TEEN PÁPIA

HE IS PRETENDING TO BE A DUCK

HE PRETENDS NOT TO BE AWARE OR
RESPONSIBLE FOR WHAT HAPPENED.

ΚΙ΄ Ο ΜΗΝΑΣ ΕΧΕΙ ΕΝΝΙΑ

ΚΙΟ΄ ΜΕΕΝΑS ΕΗΕΕ ΕΝΙΑ΄

IT'S THE 9TH OF THE MONTH

🌀 MENTIONED WHEN SOMEBODY
DOESN'T GIVE A HOOT
🌀 TO EXPRESS SOMEONES APATHY

ΠΕΡΑ ΒΡΕΧΕΙ

PÉRA VRÉHEE

IT'S RAINING FARAWAY

◎ HE DOESN'T GIVE A DARN (OR A DAMN)

◎ HE COULDN'T CARE LESS

ΧΑΡΑΣ ΤΟ ΠΡΑΓΜΑ

HARĂS TO PRÁGMA

JOY (TÓ?)THE THING ?(oh boy.)

BIG DEAL

TO SIGNIFY.... INSIGNIFICANCE OF SOMETHING

ΚΑΤΙ ΤΡΕΧΕΙ ΣΤΑ ΓΥΦΤΙΚΑ

KÁTEE TRÉHEE STA YEÉFTICA

SOMETHING IS GOING ON IN THE GYPSY AREA

◎ BIG DEAL
◎ SO WHAT?
◎ MUCH ADO ABOUT NOTHING

ΕΧΟΥΝ ΚΑΙ ΤΟΥ ΠΟΥΛΙΟΥ ΤΟ ΓΑΛΑ

ÉHOON KE TOO POOLIOÓ TO GÁLA

THEY EVEN HAVE BIRD'S MILK

THEY HAVE EVERYTHING

* *It may imply "they are rich".*

A store that has everything.

ΣΙΓΑ ΤΟΝ ΠΟΛΥΕΛΑΙΟ

SEEGÁ TON POLYÉLEO

GO SLOWLY WITH THE CHANDELIER

BIG DEAL?!!!

SO WHAT?

ΣΑΝ ΤΗΝ ΜΥΓΑ ΜΕΣ ΣΤΟ ΓΑΛΑ

SUN TIN MEÉGA MES STO GÁLA

LIKE A FLY IN THE MILK

HE-SHE-IT STICKS OUT LIKE
A SORE THUMB

ΕΙΝΑΙ ΓΙΑ ΚΛΑΜΑΤΑ

EÉNE YIÁ KLÁMATA

IT IS FOR TEARS (CRYING)

① IT IS REAL BAD
② IT IS AWFUL
③ IT IS PITIFUL

*   If you really want to get back at our waiter!! or anyone else.

ΔΕΝ ΣΦΑΞΑΝΕ

THEN SFÁKSANE

THEY HAVEN'T SLAUGHTERED

- A VERY STRONG, DETERMINED, DECIDED, DEFINITIVE BUT ALSO EMPHATIC <u>NO</u>!

- NOT ON YOUR LIFE

ΠΟΥΛΑ ΦΥΚΙΑ ΓΙΑ ΜΕΤΑΞΩΤΕΣ ΚΟΡΔΕΛΛΕΣ

POOLÁ FEÉKIA YA METAKSOTÉS CORTHÉLES

HE SELLS SEAWEED AS SILK RIBBONS

HE CHEATS

* If you ever run across this guy, don't buy fish from him.

ΑΠΟ ΠΟΥ ΚΡΑΤΑ Η ΣΚΟΥΦΙΑ ΤΟΥ

APO POO KRATÁ EE SKOÓFIA TOO

WHERE HIS CAP IS FROM

◎ WHERE HE COMES FROM

◎ WHAT HIS BACKGROUND IS

ΠΑΤΗΣΕ ΤΗΝ ΠΕΠΟΝΟΦΛΟΥΔΑ

PÁTISE TIN PEPONÓFLOOTHA*

HE STEPPED ON THE MELON PEAL

HE MADE A GROSS MISTAKE ①
HE FELL FLAT ON HIS ASS ②
Please forgive me again

* For very advanced students only. For others just "Tin patise".

ΕΙΝΑΙ ΜΕΛΙ-ΓΑΛΑ

ÉÉNE MÉLEE-GÁLA

IT IS HONEY-MILK

ⓖ EVERYTHING IS OK NOW

ⓖ LIKE NOTHING HAPPENED

AFTER A TENSE SITUATION BETWEEN TWO
PEOPLE (PERHAPS TENUOUS)

174

ΜΑΛΙΑΣΕ Η ΓΛΩΣΣΑ ΜΟΥ

MÁLIASE ĒĒ GLÓSSA MOO

MY TONGUE GREW HAIR

I TALKED TILL I WAS BLUE IN THE FACE

KOYTΣA - ΣTPABA

KOOTSÁ - STRAVÁ

LAMELY - CROOKEDLY
but also
LIMPINGLY - BLINDLY

◎ UNDER THE CIRCUMSTANCES, WE DID
OUR BEST
◎ HAPHAZARDLY
◎ HALF-ASSED (Amer.)

TOY EKANE NEPA

TOO ÉKANE NERA'

HE MADE WATERS

⊚ HE DIDN'T HOLD UP ~~THE~~ HIS END OF THE
AGREEMENT (DEAL)

⊚ THE BOAT TOOK IN WATER

ΕΓΙΝΕ Ο ΧΑΜΟΣ

ÉYEENE Ó HAMÓS

BIG ACCENT ON O

IT BECAME THE LOSS

🌀 THE PLACE WAS TURNED UPSIDE-DOWN

🌀 IT TURNED INTO A RIOT

IT CAN BE USED (A) NEGATIVE^{ly} - A CATASTROPHY

(B) POSITIVE^{ly} - GREAT FUN!

178

ΕΒΓΑΛΕ ΑΠ᾽ΤΗΝ ΜΥΓΑ ΞΥΓΚΙ

ÉVGALE APTEEN MEÉGA KSEÉGEE

HE GOT LARD OUT OF A FLY

HE IS VERY STINGY - OR TO PARAPHRASE
A BIT "HE GOT BLOOD OUT OF A TURNIP."

ΖΟΥΡΤΑ – ΦΕΡΤΑ

SOÓRTA – FÉRTA

(HAVE NO IDEA WHAT IT MEANS)

① TO AND FRO
② BACK & FORTH*
as in summer evening walks or
expressing a busybody
I JUST LIKE THE SOUND OF IT "SOORTA-FERTA"

180

ΕΦΑΓΕ ΤΑ ΜΟΥΤΡΑ ΤΟΥ

ÉFAYE TA MOÓTRA TOO

HE ATE HIS OWN FACE

HE MET WITH DISASTER BECAUSE
OF HIS OWN CARELESSNESS

ΕΦΑΓΕ Η ΦΑΚΗ ΤΟ ΛΑΔΙ

ÉFAYE EE FAKÉE TO LATHI

THE LENTIL ATE THE OIL

⊚ USED WHEN SOMETHING IS
COUNTERPRODUCTIVE

⊚ WHEN YOU PUT IN 10 DRACHMAS
AND YOU MAKE 2.

ΣΤΟ ΚΑΤΟ-ΚΑΤΟ ΤΗΣ ΓΡΑΦΗΣ

STO KÂTO-KÂTO TIS GRAFEÉS

soft g

AT THE VERY BOTTOM OF THE SCRIPT

FINALLY — THE BOTTOM LINE —

183

ΤΑ ΙΔΙΑ ΠΑΝΤΕΛΑΚΙ ΜΟΥ ΤΑ ΙΔΙΑ ΠΑΝΤΕΛΗ ΜΟΥ

ΤΟ ΙΤΗΙΑ ΡΑΝΤΕΛΑΚΙ ΜΟΟ ΤΑ ΙΤΗΙΑ ΡΑΝΤΕΛΙ ΜΟΟ

THE SAME MY LITTLE PANTELIS THE SAME MY PANTELI

◎ PEOPLE DO NOT CHANGE , NOTHING CHANGES

◎ ONCE A BITCH, ALWAYS A BITCH.

ΕΧΑΣΕ Τ'ΑΥΓΑ ΚΑΙ ΤΑ ΚΑΛΑΘΙΑ

ÉHASE TAVGÁ KE TA KALÁTHIA

HE LOST THE EGGS AND THE BASKETS

◎ HE LOST ALL HE HAD

◎ HE LOST THE WHOLE SHEBANG or
　　　　　　　　　(KIT & CABOODLE)

KOIMATE ME TIΣ KOTEΣ

KEEMÁTE ME TIS KÓTES

HE IS SLEEPING WITH THE HENS *

HE GOES TO BED VERY EARLY

* No sexual connotation.

ΕΞΩ ΑΠ᾽ΤΑ ΝΕΡΑ ΤΟΥ

ΈΚSO ΑΡΤΑ ΝΕΡΆ ΤΟΟ

OUT OF HIS WATERS

OUT OF HIS TERRITORY · UNFAMILIAR

KAΘETE ΣE ANAMENA KAPBOYNA

KÁTHETE SE ANAMÉNA KÁRVOONA

HE IS SITTING ON BURNING COAL

HE IS SITTING AT THE EDGE OF HIS SEAT

ΕΧΕΙ ΛΥΣΕΙ ΤΗΝ ΖΩΝΗ ΓΙΑ ΚΑΥΓΑ

ÉHEE LEÉSEE TIN ZÓNEE YA CAVGÁ

HE HAS UNTIED HIS BELT TO FIGHT

HE IS READY TO FIGHT

HE WENT OFF HALF COCK

ΤΡΕΙΣ ΚΙ Ο ΚΟΥΚΟΣ

TREÉS KIÓ KOOKOS

THREE AND THE CUCKOO

🌀 A THIN AUDIENCE

🌀 TO INDICATE SPARSE
ATTENDANCE AT A FUNCTION,
PERFORMANCE OR GATHERING
IN WHICH A LARGER CROWD WAS
EXPECTED

ΕΙΝΑΙ ΑΓΥΡΙΣΤΟ ΚΕΦΑΛΙ

ÉENE AΓÍRISTO KEFÁLI

HE IS AN UNTURNING HEAD

HE IS AS STUBBORN AS A MULE

ΕΙΝΑΙ ΑΡΠΑ-ΚΟΛΑ

EÉNE   ÁRPA-CÓLA *

IT IS   GRAB AND GLUE

- ⓖ IT'S SLIP-SHOD WORK
- ⓖ CATCH AS CATCH CAN   (AMER)
- ⓖ IT'S GERRY RIGGED   (AMER)

* HAS NOTHING TO DO WITH COCA or PEPSI

* To indicate the General Organization of Business, Government and things like that in Greece.

192

ΤΑ ΒΡΗΚΕ ΜΠΑΣΤΟΥΝΙΑ

TA VREÉKE BASTOÓNIA

HE FOUND THEM CANES OR
        CLUBS (as in cards)*

HE MET GREAT DIFFICULTIES

* Thorough research could not find a difinitive answer.

TA BPHKE ΣKOYPA

TA VREÉKE SKOÓRA

HE FOUND THEM DARK

HE HAD A VERY DIFFICULT TIME WITH IT

ΠΗΡΕ ΤΑ ΜΑΤΙΑ ΤΟΥ ΚΙ' ΕΦΥΓΕ

PÉERE TA MATIA TOO KIÉFIYE

HE TOOK HIS EYES AND LEFT

HE LEFT IN DISGUST

* What many Greeks do.

195

MOY THN ΔINEI

MOO TIN THEÉNEE

SHE GIVES HER TO ME

SHE UPSETS ME

ΘΑ ΣΟΥ ΔΟΣΩ ΞΥΛΟ

THA SOO THÓSO KSEÉLO

OR

ΘΑ ΦΑΣ ΞΥΛΟ

THA FAS KSEÉLO

I"LL GIVE YOU WOOD
OR
YOU'LL EAT WOOD

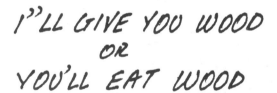 I"LL BEAT YOUR BRAINS IN (OR OUT)

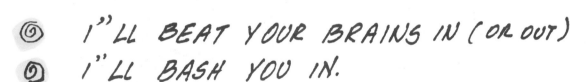 I"LL BASH YOU IN.

*   *Careful with this one too!*

ΔΕΝ ΧΑΛΑΣΕ Ο ΚΟΣΜΟΣ

THEN HÁLASE O KÓSMOS

THE WORLD WASN'T RUINED *

DON'T WORRY, THE WORLD HASN'T
COME TO AN END.

* The opposite "The world was ruined" is used to indicate (a) The world was ruined
(b) there was a catastrophy (c) we had a great time, loads of fun.

EIMAI ΠANI ME ΠANI

EÉME PANÉ ME PANÉ

I AM CLOTH WITH CLOTH

◎ I AM FLAT BROKE

◎ I DON'T HAVE TWO PENNIES TO RUB
TOGETHER

TA ΦΕΡΝΩ ΒΟΛΤΑ

TA FÉRNO VOLTA

I TURN THEM AROUND

◉ I MANAGE O.K.

◉ I MAKE DO

ΜΟΥ ΕΚΑΝΕ ΤΗΝ ΚΑΡΔΙΑ ΠΕΡΙΒΟΛΙ

MOO ÉKANE TIN KARTHIÁ PERIVÓLI

HE/SHE MADE MY HEART A GARDEN

🌀 HE DISHEARTENED ME - DISAPPOINTED ME

🌀 MADE ME FEEL BAD

ΠΙΑΣΕ ΑΒΓΟ ΚΑΙ ΚΟΥΡΕΥΤΟ

ΠΙΑΣΕ ΑΥΓΟ ΚΕ ΚΟΟΡΕΦΤΟ
PIÁSE AVGÓ KE KOÓREFTO

GET A HOLD OF AN EGG AND
GIVE IT A HAIRCUT.

TO EXPRESS FUTILITY AND
RESIGNATION

ΚΑΤΣΕ ΣΤΑ ΑΥΓΑ ΣΟΥ

KÁTΣE STAVGÁ SOO

SIT ON YOUR EGGS

① SIT·STILL / STAY PUT

② ADVISE SOMEONE NOT TO TAKE RISKS

ΦΑΤΕ ΜΑΤΙΑ ΨΑΡΙΑ ΚΑΙ ΚΟΙΛΙΑ ΠΕΡΙΔΡΟΜΟ

FÁTE MATIA PSÁRIA KE KILIÁ PERÍDROMO

THE EYES CAN EAT FISH AND THE BELLY ALL ELSE

YOO CAN LOOK ALL YOO WANT BUT YOU CAN'T TOOCH

ΠΡΟΣΕΞΕ ΤΗΝ ΣΑΝ ΤΑ ΜΑΤΙΑ ΣΟΥ

PRÓSEKSÉ TIN SUN TA MÁTIA SOO

TAKE CARE OF HER LIKE YOUR EYES

TAKE GOOD CARE OF HER

205

ΠΑΡΑ ΤΡΙΧΑ

PARÁ TREÉHA

BY A HAIR

STRAIGHT

MISSED BY A HAIR

CURLY

A CLOSE CALL

A NEAR MISS

ΦΩΣ ΦΑΝΑΡΙ

FOS - FANÁRI

LIGHT - LANTERN

· STREET LIGHT

🌀 AS CLEAR AS A BELL

🌀 CRYSTAL CLEAR

ΔΩΡΟ-ΑΔΩΡΟ

THÓRO-ÁTHORO

GIFT - NO GIFT (UNGIFT LIKE...
                        UNCOLA)

◎ INDIAN GIVER (?)(NOT SURE)

◎ GETTING NO BENEFIT FROM
   SOMETHING.

ΔΕΝ ΞΕΡΩ ΤΙ ΚΑΠΝΟ ΦΟΥΜΑΡΕΙ

THEN KSÉRO TI KAPNÓ FOUMÁREE

I DON'T KNOW WHAT KIND OF TOBACCO HE SMOKES

I DON'T KNOW WHERE HE STANDS

ΠΕΡΑΣΜΕΝΑ - ΞΕΧΑΣΜΕΝΑ

PERASMÉNA - KSEHASMÉNA

PAST EVENTS - FORGOTTEN EVENTS

ⓐ LET BYGONES BE BYGONES
ⓑ BYGONES ARE BYGONES
ⓒ THERE'S NOTHING YOU CAN DO ABOUT
THE PAST

ΜΕΡΙΔΑ ΤΟΥ ΛΕΟΝΤΟΣ

MERITHA TOO LEONTOS

THE LION'S SHARE

THE LION'S SHARE

* SURPRISE – EXACTLY THE SAME IN
BOTH LANGUAGES.

ΚΤΥΠΑ ΞΥΛΟ

ΚΤΕΈΡΑ ΚΣΕΈΛΟ

KNOCK ON WOOD

KNOCK ON WOOD

GEE. HERE'S ANOTHER ONE THATS THE SAME.
WHATSMORE IT IS USED IN THE SAME MANNER

ΟΠΟΙΟΣ ΕΧΕΙ ΜΥΓΑ ΜΥΓΙΑΖΕΤΑΙ

WHOEVER HAS A FLY IS ... FLIED
(had a very hard time with this one)
ΌΡΙΟS ΈΗΙ ΜΕΈGA, ΜΕΕΥΙΆΖΕΤΕ

WHOEVER IS GUILTY KNOWS IT

THERE IS NO SMOKE IF THERE IS NO FIRE
(Well not exactly, but what can you do?)

213

ΑΠΟΤΗΝ ΠΟΛΗ ΕΡΧΟΜΕ ΚΑΙ ΣΤΗΝ ΚΟΡΦΗ ΚΑΝΕΛΛΑ

APÓ TIN PÓLEE ÉRHOME KÉ STIN KORFÍ KANELLA

I AM COMING FROM THE CITY AND AT THE PEAK CINNAMON

- ⊚ WHAT DOES THAT HAVE TO DO WITH THE PRICE OF EGGS? (or TEA IN CHINA)
- ⊚ AN INCOHERENT, NON SENSICAL STATEMENT MEANING TO POINT OUT SOMEBODY ELSE'S INCOHERENCE AND IRRATIONALITY

ΠΡΑΣΙΝΑ ΑΛΟΓΑ

PRÁSEENA ÁLOGA

GREEN HORSES

- BALONEY - PHOOEY (AMER)
- BULLSHIT (SORRY) (AMER)
- A COCK AND BULL STORY

TPOEI TA NYXIA TOY

TRÓEE TA NEÉHIA TOO

HE IS EATING HIS FINGERNAILS

◎ HE IS VERY UPTIGHT · NERVOUS

◎ HE IS SITTING AT THE EDGE OF HIS
SEAT

ΕΜΕΙΝΕ ΜΠΟΥΚΑΛΑ

ÉMEENE BOOKALA

HE WAS LEFT A BOTTLE?

HE WAS LEFT ALONE, HE GOT

STOOD-UP

NA ΠOYME KAI TOY ΣTPABOY TO ΔIKIO

NA POÓME KE TOO STRAVOO' TO THÍKIO

TO TELL THE BLIND MAN'S JUSTICE
TO SEE THE BLIND MAN'S SIDE

ⓐ ON THE OTHER SIDE - HAND

ⓐ ON THE OTHER SIDE OF THE COIN

ΚΑΤΑ ΦΩΝΗ ΚΙ ΄ Ο ΓΑΙΔΑΡΟΣ

ΚΑΤΆ FONEE ΚΙΌ GA᷄ITHAROS

UPON THE VOICE THE DONKEY

SPEAK OF THE DEVIL!

ΣΤΗ ΧΑΣΗ ΚΑΙ ΣΤΗΝ ΦΕΞΗ

STEE HÁSEE KE STIN FÉKSI

IN THE LOSS AND IN THE LIGHT

ONCE IN A BLUE MOON

ΣΠΟΥΔΑΙΑ ΤΑ ΛΑΧΑΝΑ

SPOOTHÉA TA LÁHANA

IMPORTANT CABBAGE

BIG DEAL!

SO WHAT?

ΛΕΕΙ ΤΑ ΣΥΚΑ - ΣΥΚΑ

LÉI ΤΑ SEÉKA - SEÉKA

HE CALLS FIGS - FIGS

HE CALLS A SPADE A SPADE

ΠΝΙΓΕΤΑΙ ΣΕ ΜΙΑ ΓΟΥΛΙΑ ΝΕΡΟ

PNEÉYETE SE MIÁ GOOLIÁ NERÓ

HE DROWNS IN A SIP OF WATER

HE MAKES MOUNTAINS OUT OF MOLE HILLS

ΤΟΝ ΕΒΑΛΕ ΣΤΗ ΘΕΣΗ ΤΟΥ

TON ÉVALE STEE THÉSEE TOO

HE PUT HIM IN HIS SEAT

HE TOLD HIM WHERE TO GET OFF

TO AIMA NEPO ΔEN ΓINETAI

TO ÉMA NERÓ THEN GEÉNETE

BLOOD DOES NOT TURN INTO WATER

BLOOD IS THICKER THAN WATER

ΣΤΑ ΚΑΛΑ ΚΑΘΟΥΜΕΝΑ

STA KALÁ KATHOÓMENA

IN THE GOOD SITTINGS

OUT OF THE BLUE

ΕΠΑΘΑ ΤΗΝ ΠΛΑΚΑ ΜΟΥ

ÉPATHA TIN PLÁKA MOO

I SUFFERED MY TILE
                or MY LP

IT BLEW MY MIND

EINAI MANIKI

ÉÉNE MANEÉKEE

IT'S A SLEEVE

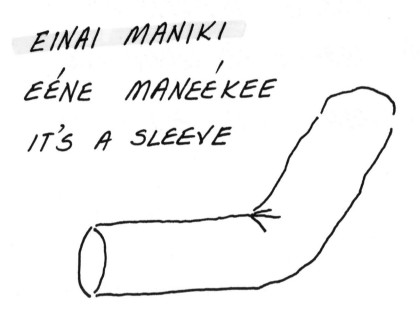

IT'S A TOUGH NUT TO CRACK

ΔΕΝ ΜΑΣΑΕΙ ΤΑ ΛΟΓΙΑ ΤΟΥ

THE MASÁEE TA LÓYIA TOO

HE DOESN'T   CHEW HIS WORDS

HE DOESN'T MINCE HIS WORDS

HE DOESN'T BEAT AROUND THE BUSH
(ABOUT)

ΕΒΑΛΕ ΤΟ ΜΑΧΑΙΡΙ ΣΤΟ ΚΟΚΑΛΟ

évane to mahéri sto kókalo

HE PUT THE KNIFE TO THE BONE

HE HIT THE NAIL ON THE HEAD.

M'ENA EMMAPO ΔYO TPYTONIA

MÉNA SBARO THIÓ TREEYÓNIA

WITH ONE SHOT TWO TURTLEDOVES

KILL TWO BIRDS WITH ONE STONE.

ΤΡΑΒΑ ΜΕ ΚΙ'ΑΣ ΚΛΑΙΩ

TRÀVA ME KIÁS KLÉO

PULL ME EVEN IF I'M CRYING

TWIST MY ARM

ΧΤΥΠΑΕΙ ΤΟ ΚΕΦΑΛΙ ΤΟΥ ΣΤΟΝ ΤΟΙΧΟ

HTEEPÁEE TO KEFÁLEE TOO STON TEÉHO

HE IS HITTING HIS HEAD ON THE WALL

◎ HE HAS REGRETS!

ΕΙΝΑΙ ΓΙΑ ΔΕΣΙΜΟ

ÉENE YIÁ THÉSEEMO

HE/SHE IS TO BE TIED

◎ HE IS NUTS
◎ HE IS CRAZY
◎ SOMETHING IS WRONG UPSTAIRS

ΚΑΠΟΙΟ ΛΑΚΚΟ ΕΧΕΙ Η ΦΑΒΑ

KÁPIO LÁKKO EHEE EE FÁVA

THERE IS A PIT (DITCH) IN THE FÁVA
(SOUP)

- SOMETHING'S FISHY
- SOMETHING'S ROTTEN IN DENMARK
- I SMELL A RAT

ΜΕ ΤΗΝ ΨΥΧΗ ΣΤΟ ΣΤΟΜΑ

ME TIN PSEEHÉE STO STÓMA

WITH HIS SOUL IN HIS MOUTH

AT THE VERY LAST MOMENT

KANEI TA ΓΛΥΚΑ MATIA

KÁNEE TA GLEEKÁ MÁTIA

HE IS MAKING SWEET EYES

HE IS MAKING EYES

ΕΙΔΕ ΤΟΝ ΧΑΡΟ ΜΕ ΤΑ ΜΑΤΙΑ ΤΟΥ

έέτηε τον Ηάρο με τα μάτια τοο

HE SAW DEATH   WITH HIS EYES

◎ HE SAW DEATH   BEFORE HIS EYES
◎ HE HAD A CLOSE CALL

ΠΗΓΕ Η ΨΥΧΗ ΜΟΥ ΣΤΗΝ ΚΟΥΛΟΥΡΗ

PEÉGE EÉ PSEEHEÉ MOO STIN KOÓLOORI

MY SOUL WENT TO COULOURI

/ WAS SCARED TO DEATH
/ WAS SCARED SHITLESS

TSIMENTO NA ΓINEI

TSIMÉNTO NA YEÉNEE

MAY IT BECOME CEMENT

TO HELL WITH IT

ΤΟΝ ΠΑΙΖΕΙ ΣΤΑ ΔΑΚΤΥΛΑ ΤΟΥ

ΤΟΝ PÉZEE STA THAKTEELÁ TOO

HE PLAYS HIM ON HIS FINGERS

HE TWISTS HIM AROUND HIS LITTLE FINGER

TON ΕΠΙΑΣΕ ΣΤΑ ΠΡΑΣΣΑ

TON ÉPIASE STA PRÁSSA

SHE CAUGHT HIM IN THE LEEKS

⊚ SHE CAUGHT HIM IN THE ACT

⊚ SHE CAUGHT HIM WITH HIS
FINGERS IN THE PIE

ΠΕΤΑΞΕ ΑΠ᾽ΤΗΝ ΧΑΡΑ ΤΗΣ

PÉTAKSE APTIN HARÁ TIS

SHE FLEW FROM HER JOY

SHE WAS TICKLED PINK (or TO DEATH)

ΠΑΤΗΣΕ ΠΟΔΙ

PÁTEESE PÓTHEE

STEPPED   FOOT

⊚ HE IMPOSED HIS WILL

⊚ HE PUT HIS FOOT DOWN

ΑΔΙΑΣΕ ΜΟΥ ΤΗΝ ΓΩΝΙΑ
ATHIASÉ MOO TIN YONIÁ
EMPTY MY CORNER

GET LOST!
BEAT IT!
SCAT! SCRAM!

ΑΛΛΟΥ Ο ΠΑΠΑΣ ΚΙ'ΑΛΛΟΥ ΤΑ ΡΑΣΑ ΤΟΥ

ALOO' O PAPAS KI'ALOO TA RASSA TOO

ELSEWHERE THE PRIEST AND ELSEWHERE
HIS ROBES
(THE PRIEST IS IN ONE PLACE AND HIS ROBES
ELSEWHERE)

ΒΟΥΛΙΑΞΑΝ   ΤΑ ΚΑΡΑΒΙΑ ΣΟΥ;

VOÓLIAKSAN   TA CARÁVIA SOO?

DID YOUR BOATS   SINK?

WHAT'S THE MATTER?

WHY DO YOU LOOK SO GLOOMY?

ΜΟΥ ΜΠΗΚΕ ΣΤΗΝ ΜΥΤΗ

ΜΟΟ ΒΕΕΚΕ STIN MEETEE

HE GOT INTO MY NOSE

◉ HE GOT ON MY NERVES
◉ HE'S DRIVING ME UP A WALL

ΕΡΡΙΞΕ ΜΑΥΡΗ ΠΕΤΡΑ ΠΙΣΩ ΤΟΥ

ÉREEKSE MÁVRI PÉTRA PÍSSO TOO

HE THREW A BLACK STONE   BEHIND HIM

HE BURNED HIS BRIDGES BEHIND HIM.

ΑΚΟΥΣΕ ΤΑ ΕΞ᾽ ΑΜΑΞΗΣ

ÁCOOSE ΤΑ ΕΧ ΑΜΑΚSΙS

HE HEARD THEM FROM THE WAGON

(CARRIAGE)

HE/SHE WAS SEVERELY REPRIMANDED

TON EKANE Φγλλο KAI Φτερο

TON ÉKANE FEÉLO KE FTERÓ

HE MADE HIM LEAF AND FEATHER

HE TOLD HIM OFF
HE DRESSED HIM DOWN

ΟΤΑΝ ΤΟΥ ΚΑΠΝΙΣΕΙ

ÓTAN TOO CAPNÍSEE

WHENEVER IT SMOKES HIM

HE'LL DO IT
WHEN HE FEELS LIKE IT.
ALSO INSTEAD OF "OTAN" YOU
MAY USE "OTI" MEANING WHATEVER
HE FEELS LIKE DOING.

ΕΓΙΝΑΝ ΑΠΟ ΔΥΟ ΧΩΡΙΑ

ÉYEENAN APÓ THIÓ HORIÁ

THEY BECAME FROM TWO VILLAGES

THEY GOT VERY ANGRY AT EACHOTHER

TON EXΩ ΣTO XEPI

TON ÉHO STO HÉREE

I'VE GOT HIM IN HAND

I'VE GOT HIM IN THE PALM OF MY HAND

KOIMATAI   OPΘIOΣ

KEEMÁTE   ORTHIOS

HE SLEEPS STANDING UP

ⓐ HE IS RATHER SLOW

ⓞ HE IS DOWNRIGHT STUPID

ⓖ HE IS NOT OPERATING WITH A FULL DECK

APON - APON
ÁRON - ÁRON
TAKE HIM - TAKE HIM

IN A HURRY

* FROM THE BIBLICAL STORY, THAT WHICH
PONTIUS PILATE SAID AFTER HE WASHED
HIS HANDS.

ΓΕΛΟΥΣΑΝ ΚΑΙ Τ' ΑΥΤΙΑ ΤΟΥ

YELOÓSAN ΚΕ ΤΑFTIÁ TOO

HIS EARS WERE LAUGHING ALSO.

HE WAS GRINNING EAR TO EAR

ΟΥΤΕ ΓΑΤΑ ΟΥΤΕ ΖΗΜΙΑ

ΟΌΤΕ ΥΆΤΑ ΟΌΤΕ ΖΕΕΜΙΆ

NO CAT NO DAMAGE

BRUSHED UNDER THE CARPET

ΚΑΠΕΤΑΝΙΟΣ ΤΟΥ ΓΛΥΚΟΥ ΝΕΡΟΥ

CAPETÁNIOS TOO YLEEKOÓ NERÓO
GLEEKOÓ

CAPTAIN OF SWEET WATER
(FRESH-WATER CAPTAIN)

TO INDICATE THAT SOMEONE (USUALLY
IN HIGH POSITION) DOES NOT KNOW WHAT
HE IS DOING.

KATI ΠHPE T'AYTI MOY

CÁTI PEÉRE TAFTÍ MOO

SOMETHING TOOK MY EAR

I HEARD SOMETHING ABOUT IT.

ΚΟΨΕ ΛΑΣΠΗ

KÓPSE LÁSPI

CUT MUD

GET LOST
SCRAM!

ME TO NI KAI ME TO ΣΙΓΜΑ

MEH TO NÉE KE MEH TO SIGMA

WITH AN "N" AND AN "S"

WITH EVERY MINUTE DETAIL

262

ΤΟΥ ΑΝΟΙΞΕ ΤΑ ΜΑΤΙΑ

TOO ÁNEEKSE TA MÁTIA

HE/ OPENED HIS EYES
/SHE

 HE/SHE LET HIM IN ON IT

(INFORMED or EDUCATED HIM)

ΤΡΩΕΙ ΤΑ ΝΥΧΙΑ ΤΟΥ

TRÓEE TA NEÉHIA TOO

HE IS EATING HIS NAILS

◎ HE IS VERY NERVOUS, TENSE

◎ HE IS SITTING ON HOT COALS

ΕΠΕΣΕ ΑΠΟ ΤΑ ΣΥΝΝΕΦΑ

ÉPESE APÓ TA SEÉNEFA

HE FELL FROM THE CLOUDS

Ⓖ IT HIT HIM LIKE A THUNDERBOLT
(A TON OF BRICKS)

Ⓖ IT CAME AS A SURPRISE

265

ΧΑΙΡΕΤΑ ΜΑΣ ΤΟΝ ΠΛΑΤΑΝΟ

HERÉTA MAS TON PLATANO

SAY GOOD-BYE TO THE MAPLE TREE
(PLANE TREE?)

TO INDICATE A LOST CAUSE OR A
LONG DELAY DURING WHICH NOTHING
GETS DONE

ΑΝΟΙΞΕ ΤΗΝ ΚΑΡΔΙΑ ΤΟΥ

ÁNEEKSE TIN CARDIÁ TOO

HE OPENED HIS HEART

 HE OPENED UP TO SOMEONE

 HE TALKED CANDIDLY ABOUT EVERYTHING
THAT HE FELT

AND NOW A BONUS SECTION - NOT EVEN
ON THE TABLE OF CONTENTS — OF SMALL
BUT VERY-VERY HELPFUL SOUNDS.

SOUNDS ARE VERY IMPORTANT IN GREEK

EVERYDAY COMMUNICATION. I DON'T KNOW

WHY NOR DO I KNOW HOW THEY DEVELOPED

OR FOR THAT MATTER WHERE THEY CAME

FROM EVEN THOUGH I ASKED SEVERAL PEOPLE.

ΠΟ ΠΟ ΠΟ ΠΟ ΠΟ ΠΟ ΠΟ ΠΟ

PO PO PO PO PO PO PO ΠΟ

<u>INST</u> ACCENT ON FIRST PO AND THEN TRAILING

DEPENDING ON THE EMPHASIS YOU
INCREASE OR DECREASE THE NUMBER OF POS

◎ YOU DON'T SAY
◎ NO KIDDING?
◎ JESUS
◎ NO S--T?!

BAD :PO-PO
WORSE:PO-PO-PO
REAL BAD :PO POPO PO PO
WORST : PO PO PO POPO PO PO PO
TERRIBLE: PO AD INFINITUM

270

ΠΑ ΠΑ ΠΑ ΠΑ ΠΑ

ΠΑ PA PA PA PA PA

PA PA PA PA PA

⊚ NO WAY
⊚ NEVER

TO SHOW DISAPPROVAL OR DISLIKE
THE MORE THE PAS THE GREATER
THE   DISLIKE. HATE = 1.236 PAs

PE

REh

CAN'T TRANSLATE IT

REh IS AN EXTRAORDINARY SOUND. EVEN
THOUGH IT IS NOT USED IN POLITE, FORMAL
CONVERSATIONS YOU COME ACCROSS IT ALMOST
CONSTANTLY. SOMETIMES IT IS LIKE THE
AMERICAN "HEY". PE ΣΥ - RÉSÍ = HEY YOU
PE ΓΙΩΡΓΟ - RE YIORGO = HEY GEORGE
A VARIATION OF IT IS BPE - VRÉh.
MOST LIKELY, THEY TELL ME, OF TURKISH ORIGIN.

MΠA

BĀh or BAA (The same)

NOT UNLIKE THE SHEEP SOUND
GENERALLY IT HAS TWO MEANINGS:

A - BĀ? (Rather short)(with a questioning
accent) = Is that right?
= It's news to me.

B BĀĀĀ (Long) = NO
= I don't think so

E ;

Eh ?

what?

JUST A PLAIN Eh WILL DO. NOT EXTREMELY
POLITE DO NOT USE IN FORMAL CONVERSATION
EVEN IF THE CHANCE MAY BE SLIM.
what did you say?
can you repeat ?

Oʊ   (OʊOʊOʊOʊOʊ)

OO   as in t<u>oo</u>   OOOOOO

YES!

A VERY DEFINITE YES. THE LONGER THE OOOO
THE MORE DEFINITE THE YES
THIS SOUND IS USUALLY (BUT NOT ALWAYS)
FOLLOWED BY A CLOCKWISE MOTION OF THE
RIGHT ARM SEMI RAISED, PALM SEMI OPEN.

* Careful! Counter-clockwise motion means go backwards in space-time e.t.c.

another BONUS section on necessary...

PEJORATIVES

* mild
** not so mild
*** adventurous
**** rigorously adventurous
***** down-right obscene° {M ------}
                                {P ------}

° DUE TO THE AUTHOR'S TIMIDITY AND GOOD
BREEDING THIS PUBLICATION CONTAINS NO
FIVE STAR PEJORATIVES.

ΕΙΣΑΙ ΣΤΡΑΒΟΞΥΛΟ   * * ✗

ÉÉSE STRAVÓKSEELO

YOU ARE A CROOKED WOOD
               (BENT WOOD)

◎ YOU ARE DIFFICULT TO DEAL WITH
◎ YOU ARE IMPOSSIBLE TO DEAL WITH
◎ NO REASONABLE HUMAN BEING CAN
    POSSIBLY GET ALONG WITH YOU.

EINAI TENEKEΣ ✳⌄

EÉNE TENEKES

HE IS A TIN

HE IS WORTHLESS, DISHONEST
UNTRUSTWORTHY AND BESIDES
HE IS NO GOOD.

TON KAKO ZOY TON KAIPO *＊＊≁

TON KAKÓ SOO TON KERÓ

YOUR BAD WEATHER (TIME?)

ⓖ MAY YOU HAVE A BAD TIME
              or simply

ⓖ GO TO HELL

*   Use it gently and only when extremely annoyed. (Inflamatory)

ΕΙΣΑΙ ΚΑΚΟΣ, ΣΤΡΑΒΟΣ ΚΙ' ΑΝΑΠΟΔΟΣ ***
(or ΨΥΧΡΟΣ)

EESE KAKOS, STRAVOS, KIANAPOTHOS
(or PSEEHROS)

YOU ARE BAD, CROOKED AND BACKWARDS
or COLD

STRAVOS = also blind

ANAPOTHOS = also INSIDE-OUT or UPSIDE-DOWN

YOU ARE A MISERABLE HUMAN BEING (S.O.B) *

* USE IT CAUTIOUSLY AND ONLY IF YOU ARE BIGGER
THAN HE/SHE

282

1- ΕΙΣΑΙ ΓΑΙΔΑΡΟΣ
   EESE   GAEETHAROS
   YOU ARE A DONKEY

2- ΕΙΣΑΙ ΖΩΟΝ
   EESE   ZÓON
   YOU ARE AN ANIMAL

3- ΕΙΣΑΙ ΓΟΥΡΟΥΝΙ
   EESE GOOROÓNI
   YOU ARE A PIG

* * ∿
2½ STAR PEJORATIVES
MEANING ROUGHLY THE SAME
THING. DONKEY = STUBBORN
           PIG = UNCIVILIZED
     ANIMAL = ALL OF THE
     ABOVE. FOR THE
     SAKE OF DIRECTNESS
     AND BREVITY EESE
     IS FREQUENTLY
     OMITTED

ΚΟΥΝΙΑ ΠΟΥ ΣΕ ΚΟΥΝΑΓΕ   *

COÓNIA POO SE COÓNAYE

CRADLE THAT CRADLED YOU

YOU ARE FULL OF IT !
(you don't expect me to believe you.)

284

TO MYAΛO ΣOY KAI MIA ΛIPA   *

TO MIALÓ SOO KE MIÁ LEÉRA

YOUR BRAIN AND A GOLDEN SOVEREIGN

ⓐ ARE YOU NUTS?
ⓑ SURELY YOU SOUND LIKE A SIMPLETON
THIS, HAS SOME MORE TO IT BUT I DON'T
REMEMBER IT

ΕΙΣΑΙ ΤΟΥΒΛΟ **

ÉÉSE TOÓVLO

YOU ARE A BRICK!

🌀 YOU HAVE THE I.Q. OF A BRICK!
🌀 YOU ARE IGNORANT!
🌀 YOU ARE MENTALLY DEFICIENT!
🌀 YOU ARE AN IDIOT!!!

* Careful with this one too!

ΕΙΣΑΙ ΝΤΟΥΒΑΡΙ   **

ÉESE DOOVÁRI

YOU ARE A WALL

🌀 YOU ARE IGNORANT

🌀 YOU ARE A SLOW LEARNER - RETARDED - STUPID*

* *Not a subtle indication that you are seriously questioning one's intellectual capacity.*

287

ΜΟΥ ΕΓΙΝΕΣ ΣΤΕΝΟΣ ΚΟΡΣΕΣ *

MOO ÉYEENES STENÓS CORSÉS

YOU'VE BECOME A TIGHT GIRDLE

 YOU ARE A PEST

 YOU ARE A PAIN IN THE NECK

 YOU ARE BUGGING THE HELL OUT OF ME

THE FRIENDLY AND HOSPITABLE FACES OF GREECE

JOHN (YIÁNNIS)
THE BAKER.

YIANNIS
THE TAVERNA
OWNER

YIANNIS
THE KIOSK
OWNER

YIANNIS

YIANNIS
THE TAVERNA SITTER

YIANNIS
THE FISHERMAN

MORE FACES*
(Y)
ALL GIANNISES
AND ONE GEORGE

KOMBOLOI

*SOME NOT SO FRIENDLY

TO KAMAKI
(ASK)

290

EVEN THOUGH PROVERBS FALL IN AN ENTIRELY DIFFERENT CATEGORY,* THE FOLLOWING JUST MAY BE PROVERBS YET THEY MAY NOT BE. OF 63 PEOPLE I ASKED THE ANSWERS WERE ALMOST 50-50 BUT THEN AGAIN IT IS VIRTUALLY IMPOSSIBLE FOR GREEKS TO AGREE ON ANYTHING. IT IS JUST PART OF THEIR CHARM.

*THE AUTHOR HAS CONSIDERED ANOTHER WORK WITH PROVERBS, IT COULD BE FUN BUT TOO STRENUOUS FOR THE TIME BEING.

TO KAΠO TO ΠAΛIKAΡI ΞEPEI KI'AΛΛO MONOΠATI

TO KALÓ TO PALICÁRI KSÉRI KIÁLO MONOPÁTI

THE CLEVER YOUNG MAN KNOWS MANY PATHS
(ANOTHER WAY)

THERE IS MORE THAN ONE WAY TO SKIN A CAT

Ο ΚΑΠΟΣΟ ΚΑΠΕΤΑΝΙΟΣ ΣΤΗΝ ΦΟΥΡΤΟΥΝΑ ΦΑΙΝΕΤΑΙ

O KALÓS O KAPETÁNIOS STIN FOORTOÓNA FÉNETE

THE GOOD CAPTAIN PROVES HIMSELF IN THE STORM

SELF EXPLANATORY. THE MEANING IS
TRANSFERED TO MANY OTHER SITUATIONS

ΑΛΛΑΞΕ Ο ΜΑΝΩΛΙΟΣ, ΕΒΑΛΕ ΤΑ ΡΟΥΧΑ ΤΟΥ ΑΛΛΟΙΩΣ

ALAKSE O MANOLIÓS, ÉVALE TA ROÓHA TOO ALIÓS

MANOLIOS CHANGED, HE WORE HIS CLOTHES
DIFFERENTLY

PEOPLE DON'T CHANGE

ΤΩΡΑ ΣΤΑ ΓΕΡΑΜΑΤΑ ΜΑΘΕ ΓΕΡΟ ΓΡΑΜΜΑΤΑ

TÓRA STA YERÁMATA MÁTHE YÉRO GRÁMATA

NOW IN YOUR OLD AGE, OLD MAN, LEARN TO READ
(and write)

YOU CAN'T TEACH AN OLD DOG NEW TRICKS

TA ΠΟΛΛΑ ΛΟΓΙΑ ΕΙΝΑΙ ΦΤΩΧΙΑ

TA POLÁ LÓYIA EÉNAI FTÓHIA

TOO MUCH TALK IS POVERTY

ΛΟΓΙΑ ΛΟΓΙΑ ΛΟΓΙΑ ΛΟΓΙΑ ΛΟΓΙΑ ΛΟΓΙΑ ΛΟΓΙΑ ΛΟΓΙΑ ΛΟΓΙΑ ΛΟΓΙΑ ΛΟΓΙΑ ΛΟΓΙΑ ΛΟΓΙΑ ΛΟΓΙΑ ΛΟΓΙΑ ΛΟΓΙΑ ΛΟΓΙΑ ΛΟΓΙΑ ΛΟΓΙΑ

ACTIONS SPEAK LOUDER THAN WORDS
(By approximation in meaning)

ΘΕΛΕΙ ΤΗΝ ΠΙΤΑ ΟΛΟΚΛΗΡΗ
ΚΑΙ ΤΟΝ ΣΚΥΛΟ ΧΟΡΤΑΤΟ

THÉLI TIN PÉETA OLÓKLEERI
KE TON SKEÉLO HORTATO

HE WANTS THE PIE WHOLE
AND THE DOG FULL
HE WANTS HIS CAKE AND EAT IT TOO

ΤΟ ΜΗΛΟ ΠΕΦΤΕΙ ΚΑΤΩ ΑΠ ΤΗΝ ΜΗΛΙΑ

ΤΟ ΜΕΕΛΟ ΡΕΦΤΙ ΚΑΤΟ ΑΡΤΙΝ ΜΕΕΛΙΑ

THE APPLE FALLS UNDER THE APPLETREE

A CHIP OFF OF THE OLD BLOCK

Η ΑΛΕΠΟΥ ΕΚΑΤΟ ΤΟ ΑΛΕΠΟΥΔΑΚΙ ΕΚΑΤΟΝΕΙΚΟΣΙ

Ε Ε ΑΛΕΡΟΎ ΕΚΑΤΟ΄ ΤΟ ΑΛΕΡΟΟΘΗΑΚΙ ΕΚΑΤΟΝΕΕΚΟΣΙ

THE FOX ONE HUNDRED THE BABY FOX 120

TO EXPLAIN THAT YOUTH'S ARROGANCE
IS JUST THAT AND NO MORE. HOW CAN
A YOUNG PERSON BE WISER THAN AN
OLD ONE?

ΠΗΓΕ ΓΙΑ ΜΑΛΙ ΚΑΙ ΒΓΗΚΕ ΚΟΥΡΕΜΕΝΟΣ

PÉEGE YA MALÉE KE VGEÉKE KOOREMÉNOS

(wool?)

HE WENT FOR HAIR AND CAME OUT WITH

A HAIRCUT

HE DID SOMETHING FOR GAIN BUT HE
CAME OUT A LOSER

300

ΤΙ ΕΧΕΙΣ ΓΙΑΝΝΗ; ΤΙ ΕΙΧΑ ΠΑΝΤΑ

TEE ÉHIS YIÁNNI? TI EÉHA PÁNTA

WHAT DO YOU HAVE JOHN? WHAT I ALWAYS
HAD

THIS DESCRIBES (NEGATIVELY) A STATIC
SITUATION, A COMPLAINING PERSON e.t.c.

ΕΚΑΨΕ ΤΗΝ ΚΑΛΥΒΑ ΤΟΥ ΝΑ ΜΗΝ ΤΟΝ ΤΡΩΝ ΟΙ ΨΥΛΛΟΙ

ÉKAPSE TIN KALÉEVA TOO NA MÍN TON TRON EE PSEELI

HE BURNED DOWN HIS HOUSE SO THAT THE FLEAS
WOULDN'T BITE HIM

HE BIT OFF HIS NOSE TO SPITE HIS FACE

ΚΑΛΙΟ ΑΡΓΑ ΠΑΡΑ ΠΟΤΕ

KÁLIO APGÁ PARÁ POTÉ

BETTER LATE THAN NEVER

(CAN'T PUT IT ANY BETTER)

AFTERTHOUGHTS

WELL, WE'VE COME TO THE END. ACTUALLY I HAVE FOUND SEVERAL MORE BUT MY HAND IS TIRED AND I JUST DON'T HAVE THE AMBITION TO WORK ON THEM. FORGIVE ME. I HOPE YOU'VE BEEN AMUSED A BIT AT THE STRANGE & UNIQUE WAYS PEOPLE USE THEIR LANGUAGE AND REMEMBER WHAT LILLY TOMLIN SAID: "EVEN IF YOU WIN THE RAT-RACE, YOU'RE STILL A RAT." SO, WHY GET INTO IT IN THE FIRST PLACE? AS FOR ME I AM OFF TO FLY MY KITE. THANKS.

Vernon Vas Elliott is an unorthodox, eccentric sort of individual who laughs at things most others don't. He is fascinated by strange, inexplicable trivia and has made a thorough and remarkable study which took him the best part of half an hour, of wise old adages and phrases, the origins of which are lost in antiquity not to mention ancient times. This is probably the only book he will ever write, returning upon its completion to his favourite freedoms of wasting time sunsets and kite flying.

Vernon is a peculiar and eccentric sort of a guy who laughs randomly and constantly smokes his pipe. He is fascinated by odd and strange linguistic phenomena and in 25 years he has made an inconsequential and forgetable research on weird things people say. This is his first unplanned book which contains a number of debatable translations. He wrote it, in his kitchen, between kite flying expeditions an activity which he has returned to full time, thank goodness.

His only claim to fame is that his second cousin wrote a great book at 23

* THIS IS NOT A MISTAKE! WE JUST COULDN'T MAKE UP OUR MINDS WHICH BIO TO USE, SO WE USED BOTH!

*   He doesn't really look like this but he would like to

307

ABOUT THE AUTHOR'S FRIENDS AND RELATIVES

SADLY, THE AUTHOR HAS NEVER MET MOST OF HIS FRIENDS. SOME OF THEM, MARK TWAIN BERTRAND RUSSELL, HENRY DAVID THOREAU ARE GONE, OTHERS LIKE WOODY ALLEN, LILLY TOMLIN, DAVE BARRY ARE FAR AWAY. MOST OF THOSE WHO KNOW HIM HOWEVER, LIKE HIM BECAUSE HE RARELY SAYS ANYTHING.

ALL OF HIS RELATIVES, EXCEPT HIS MOTHER, HAVE TOTALLY DISASSOCIATED THEMSELVES FROM HIM AND CLAIM NOT TO KNOW HIM, EVEN WHEN NOT ASKED.

NOTED CRITICS SAY...

◉ MR. ELLIOTT SHOULD CONFINE HIS WRITING TO POST-CARDS TO HIS MOTHER FROM FAR AWAY PLACES (PREFERABLY.)   *The Gazzette*

◉ HIS SISTER WILL POSSIBLY BUY THE BOOK.   *Voice*

◉ MR. ELLIOTT'S HUMOR IS ONLY EXCEEDED BY HIS MODESTY, OF WHICH HE HAS NONE   *Zilch Fromme*

◉ WHO IS THIS ELLIOTT AND WHY IS HE MAKING FUN OF US?   *Petros Diacopanagiotakopoulos*

◉ I AM CERTAINLY GLAD HE WENT BACK TO KITES
                    — *Vas Vernon Elliott - His father*

ALL THE GREEK YOU"LL EVER NEED
and more.

BY THE SAME AUTHOR

1. GREEK - A FRACTURED LEXICON
   Over 300 idioms, phrases, pejoratives as well as
   sounds, absolutely necessary to communicate in Greek
   or even to amuse yourself.

2. A VISITORS GUIDE TO MODERN GREEK BEHAVIOR AND HABITS
   A tongue-in-cheek approach to the culture
   shock.

3. A VISITORS GUIDE TO GREEK DRIVING? AND OTHER OXYMORA
   AND PARADOXA
   1001 things a visitor needs to know in
   order to survive, or just to laugh.

Mr Elliot has authored several other works which, however, no publisher has
dared as yet to accept.

ORDER FORM

PLEASE MAIL TO --
        name

   AT --
        address

----
  city   state   zip

	How many	times ea.	total
GREEK: A FRACTURED LEXIKON	--------------	------------	---------
GREEK BEHAVIOR AND HABITS	--------------	------------	---------
GREEK DRIVING	--------------	------------	---------
ADD HANDLING & POSTAGE	--------------	------------	---------
GRAND TOTAL			---------

VISA - M.C. - AMEX - CHECK - M.O. ---
             credit card number

SPECIAL WHOLESALE PRICES AVAILABLE ON REQUEST FOR LARGE ORDERS FOR CHURCH FUNDRAISERS, BOOK STORES, TRAVEL AGENCIES E.T.C.

mail to:

REGENT

2950 North U.S. 41
Naples, Florida
33940

tel. (813) 263-6622